THE RUSSIAN PROVINCE AFTER COMMUNISM

Also by Vincent Edwards

HUNGARY SINCE COMMUNISM: The Transformation of Business
(*with György Bögel and Marian Wax*)

MANAGEMENT CHANGE IN EAST GERMANY
(*with Peter Lawrence*)

Also by Gennady Polonsky

MANAGING THE TRANSITION (*in Slovak*)

Also by Avgust Polonsky

ENTREPRENEURIAL SYSTEMS OF MANAGEMENT (*in Russian*)

SOCIO-ECONOMIC PROBLEMS OF LABOUR COLLECTIVES
(*in Russian*)

The Russian Province after Communism

Enterprise Continuity and Change

Vincent Edwards
Professor of East European Management and Culture
Buckinghamshire Business School
Buckinghamshire Chilterns University College
England

Gennady Polonsky
Reader in Transitional Economics
Buckinghamshire Business School
Buckinghamshire Chilterns University College
England

and

Avgust Polonsky
Professor of Sociology
Volgograd State Academy of Architecture
Volgograd
Russia

HC
340.12
.Z7
V6736
2000

First published in Great Britain 2000 by
MACMILLAN PRESS LTD
Houndmills, Basingstoke, Hampshire RG21 6XS and London
Companies and representatives throughout the world

A catalogue record for this book is available from the British Library.

ISBN 0–333–73410–6

First published in the United States of America 2000 by
ST. MARTIN'S PRESS, INC.,
Scholarly and Reference Division,
175 Fifth Avenue, New York, N.Y. 10010

ISBN 0–312–22095–2

Library of Congress Cataloging-in-Publication Data
Edwards, Vincent, 1947–
The Russian province after communism : enterprise continuity and
change / Vincent Edwards, Gennady Polonsky, Avgust Polonsky.
p. cm.
Includes bibliographical references and index.
ISBN 0–312–22095–2 (cloth)
1. Volgogradskaia oblast' (Russia)—Economic conditions. 2. Post
-communism—Economic aspects—Russia (Federation)—Volgogradskaia
oblast'. 3. Volgogradskaia oblast' (Russia)—Commerce.
4. Industrial management—Russia (Federation)—Volgogradskaia
oblast'. I. Polonsky, Gennady, 1957– . II. Polonsky, Avgust,
1934– . III. Title.
HC340.12.Z7V6736 1999
330.947'47086—dc21   98–32037
                                                                 CIP

This book is printed on paper suitable for recycling and made from fully managed and
sustained forest sources.

10 9 8 7 6 5 4 3 2 1
09 08 07 06 05 04 03 02 01 00

Printed and bound in Great Britain by
Antony Rowe Ltd, Chippenham, Wiltshire

Contents

List of Tables

Preface

Momentous changes have engulfed Russia over the past decade: fundamental system change in politics and economics; the independence of the former 'satellite' states of Central and Eastern Europe; and the disintegration of the Union of Soviet Socialist Republics (USSR). Rigid central control of political and economic activities as well as of individuals' private lives has yielded to political democracy, free market economics and individual liberty – many commentators would add that it has added to licence and criminality too. There is no doubt, however, that Russia has experienced substantial change.

Much of the reporting of the changes has focused understandably on Moscow and to a certain degree on other major cities such as St Petersburg. The impact of change has, however, encompassed all of Russia. One aspect of the research project was to explore the situation in provincial Russia, away from the limelight of the main centres of political and economic activity. Hence, at least in part, the choice of Volgograd, in south-east Russia, as our research site.

The repercussions of the change of economic system have of necessity affected companies and their managers. The formerly centralized organization of economic activities has by and large gone. What has replaced it? How have companies and their managers responded? What is the context in which companies are now operating? How much or how little has changed? These are some of the questions for which we sought answers in the Russian province a decade after 'improvements to socialism' were first mooted.

STRUCTURE OF THE BOOK

The structure of the book is as follows: Chapter 1 describes the overall purpose of the research that was undertaken. Chapter 2 explores the broader economic, political and social contexts of Volgograd and its oblast since the mid-1980s. Chapter 3 investigates the current situation from the perspective of its historical evolution. Chapters 4–7 are based on our investigations of companies, each chapter focusing on a different category of company (not including criminal organizations). Chapter 8 presents the results of a survey of managers in two of Volgograd's industrial enterprises. Chapter 9 comprises a general analysis of the situation of companies resulting from the transformation process, and Chapter 10 presents more general conclusions of the study, as well as attempting a prognosis of future developments.

Acknowledgements

The data for this book would have been extremely difficult to collect without the support of many individuals in Volgograd, working in companies, working in local government and public administration and working for themselves. The authors are most grateful for the support they all gave.

We are also grateful to those individuals whom we happened to meet and engage in conversation. Whatever the weakness of anecdotal evidence, it can help to add colour and flavour to the more structured collection of data.

Finally we would like to thank Buckinghamshire Business School for providing the financial support which made journeys to Volgograd possible, and for the general encouragement it gives to the activities of the Centre for Research into East European Business.

Part I
Background and Context

1 Research Issues

Nearly everyone who has ever traveled to Russia has become an expert, and nearly every expert cancels out every other expert.
(Steinbeck, 1994 [1949]:178)

Why Volgograd? This question was asked on a number of occasions by Russians whom we had approached to assist us with our research. It was also a question we had asked ourselves. Why travel over 1000 kilometres (600 miles) to the south-east of Moscow to conduct research in a large industrial city? What could be the purpose? What might be the outcomes?

A combination of circumstances brought the research team together. Firstly, two of the team had close connections with the city, knowing it and its enterprises well. Avgust Polonsky has lived in Volgograd since 1976 and is professor of sociology at the Academy of Architecture. Gennady Polonsky lived in the city between 1976 and 1987 and has made frequent return visits since. In 1992 he became senior lecturer in economics at Buckinghamshire Business School (BBS) and is a member of its Centre for Research into East European Business (CREEB). Vincent Edwards teaches strategic management at BBS and is a founder member of CREEB. Research into the economic transformation of Central and Eastern Europe and Russia is a staple component of CREEB's activities.

The idea to do research in Russia was, moreover, not purely opportunistic, even though seizing opportunities was a necessary condition of our research as we will explain more fully later.

CREEB has followed closely developments in Central and Eastern Europe since the early 1990s and has concluded a range of studies in the countries of the region. Russia, however, is by far the largest country hitherto which has experienced the collapse of communism. The collapse of communism has had far-reaching consequences in the political, economic and social spheres. Each of the countries of Central and Eastern Europe has tackled the transformation in a different way and has resolved its difficulties to varying degrees. Russia, however, is different in many respects from these other countries, many of whose inhabitants perceived the collapse of communism as a liberation from an alien system.

Russia may be considered different from the countries of Central and Eastern Europe in that:

- it is far larger in area (just over 17 million square kilometres) and population (close to 150 million), stretching from the Arctic in the north to the Caucasus and the Mongolian and Chinese borders in the south, from the Baltic enclave around Kaliningrad in the west to around 100 kilometres (60 miles) from both Alaska and the northern Japanese island of Hokkaido in the east;

- communism had prevailed in Russia since 1917, far longer than in any other state and was accordingly closely associated with Russia. The communist system was predominantly a Russian creation, implemented in the Soviet Union by Lenin and exported by Stalin to Central and Eastern Europe;

- the system, as Russia was communist for over 70 years, became more strongly ingrained than elsewhere, largely obliterating recollections of a pre-communist heritage which might be utilized to revitalize the present;

- the collapse of communism has gone hand in hand with the break-up of the Soviet Union. Russia is substantially smaller than the Soviet Union had been, and this dissolution of the Soviet Union has been experienced by many Russians as a diminution of Russia's prestige and standing in the world. The former superpower, which for decades had been intent on challenging the United States in the political, military and economic spheres, is now undergoing a period of disarray in many fields;

- Russia's sheer size may be an impediment to transformation as the former levers of centralized power have loosened substantially, encouraging centrifugal forces to assert themselves and create local bases of political and economic power.

To do research in Russia is more than a mere replication of work carried out elsewhere. A major driver for the research was the authors' interest in delving more deeply into the process of transformation currently going on in Russia. The research was driven above all by intellectual curiosity, a desire to find out and understand what was happening in Russia outside the major centres of Moscow and St Petersburg, both of which have featured heavily in the news media and other publications. The authors were of the view that there is already substantial information on Russia's two major cities. These have grabbed the main attention abroad and have also attracted the lion's share of foreign direct investment (FDI). According to former Russian prime minister Victor Chernomyidin, 57 per cent of all FDI in Russia, which is low in absolute terms and even lower in per-capita terms when compared to countries such as Hungary and Poland, has been made in Moscow; about 7 per cent in St Petersburg; and slightly more than 5 per cent in Tyumen oblast (*Finansovye izvestia*, 15 November 1997). However, around 85 per cent of the Russian population live outside these areas. This other Russia, which features far less frequently and consistently, was considered far more likely to provide a more balanced picture of post-communist transformation. The authors hence decided to designate their project as transformation in the Russian province.

Some of our Russian counterparts took issue with the term 'province', expressing the view that the word has derogatory connotations. We replied that we had chosen the word 'province' in a purely neutral sense as a contrast to Russia's two main urban centres, and in no way intended any offence.

Why Volgograd? The authors felt that Volgograd would be an appropriate research site for a number of reasons:

- Volgograd, with around one million inhabitants, is a substantial urban and industrial centre and the capital of Volgograd oblast. Under communism it was the location of numerous large enterprises producing a variety of industrial and other goods. It has continued to act as a substantial industrial centre. Its function as the oblast capital also endows the city with certain characteristics as the location of city and provincial governments and as a centre for local political and economic decision making.

- In contrast, Volgograd province (Volgogradskaja oblast) is predominantly agricultural and a significant producer of grain and fodder. This diversity of economic activity permitted the study of developments both in industry and agriculture.

- Volgograd has considerable symbolic significance in Russia's recent history as the site of the battle of Stalingrad* (1942–3) which with the defeat of the German army is generally considered the turning point of the Second World War in Europe. The city's location on the Volga, the river central to Russian life and thought, adds a further symbolic dimension as a consequence of numerous historical and cultural associations which have been explored with sensitivity and imagination by Chamberlain (1995).

• Volgograd is more than 1000 kilometres from Moscow and is closer to Kazakhstan, the Ukraine and the Caucasus. In this respect the study enables the authors to explore the relationship between the centre (Moscow) and one of Russia's more peripheral regions, as well as the local relationships between the city and its region.

• At the same time Volgograd's role as a major inland port on the River Volga creates a link with the wider world. The Volga provides a link to both Moscow and other major urban centres. Upstream of Volgograd are the major industrial cities of Saratov, Samara, Kazan and Nizhni Novgorod. Downstream is Astrakhan. Just beyond Astrakhan the Volga enters the Caspian Sea, the world's largest fresh-water lake, the waters of which are shared by Russia, the former Soviet republics of Azerbaijan, Kazakhstan and Turkmenistan and by Iran. Moreover, the Volga–Don Canal, which meets the Volga in the vicinity of the city, permits access to the Sea of Azov and from there to the Black Sea.

Whilst having an identity of their own, Volgograd and its region clearly share many similarities with other cities and regions in Russia. Volgograd is in many respects an 'average' Russian province. The statistics relating to industrialization, income levels and the incidence of economic activity for military purposes indicate that Volgograd is around the average for Russia. In agriculture, too, Volgograd oblast has been described as a 'microcosm of Russian agriculture in three respects' – land use, negative consequences of soil improvement measures and general coverage of soil and climatic zones (Brock,

---

* The city was founded in the latter part of the sixteenth century and was originally named Tsaritsyn; it was renamed Stalingrad in 1925 and subsequently Volgograd in 1961.

1994). Politically, too, Volgograd is one of the majority of still 'red' regions in Russia in that more than half of the governors of the oblasti and their equivalents still declare themselves as communists or have been elected with communist support.

The waves of the impact of transformation have washed across Russia. That is not to say that different locations have not responded differently, that local conditions have not manifested considerable variation. However, all areas have had to react and respond to the same general trends of changing political and economic systems.

RESEARCH QUESTIONS

In undertaking research on Volgograd we intended to seek answers to a series of questions relating to the transformation which Russia has been experiencing since the mid-1980s and more specifically since the collapse of communism.

Whilst the focus of the research was primarily on the changes affecting the economic sector, the authors decided that such changes – both at the macroeconomic level and at the level of individual enterprises and their managers and employees – could be properly understood only if the changes were related to parallel changes in the political and social spheres. This position is in accord with the views of Vladimir Mau and Vadim Stupin (1997), according to whom 'an adequate assessment of economic processes on the regional as well as the federal level – and especially under conditions of acute social shifts – cannot be based exclusively on purely economic parameters' (p. 6). Mau and Stupin accordingly propose the investigation of 'economic, social and political processes in combination and interaction' (p. 7).

The authors therefore decided to investigate the evolution of individual firms in the context of the changing political and social contexts, as the change of political system has had far-reaching consequences for economic activities, social conditions as well as political life itself.

The project was therefore designed to address a range of issues, more specifically:

- How had enterprises been affected by the change of economic system? How had they responded to the disappearance of the former system of economic management? What were they doing to survive and prosper in the new environment? What was the position of enterprises with regard to products and markets, both for inputs and sales? What have been the implications for organization and employment? What mechanisms have enterprises evolved to come to terms with the manifold problems afflicting them?

- Who were the enterprise leaders? What were their backgrounds and how had they achieved their current positions? What was the relationship between management and ownership? What were the distinguishing characteristics of these enterprise leaders?

- Was there a new relationship between the economic and political spheres? What was the relationship between the city and oblast administrations and the enterprises in the locality? To what extent did local and regional politicians feel able to assist enterprises and local economic development? To what extent was the influence of Moscow still felt?

- How had the panoply of changes impacted on the lives of ordinary people? What had been the effect on the employment and remuneration of individuals, on their social well-being and on their state of health?

FIRST IMPRESSIONS

First impressions of Volgograd indicated that there would be no easy answers to many of these questions. In many ways the external appearance of Volgograd had changed little since 1990. Statues of Lenin still abound. The centre of the city is well laid out and its condition is little different from centres in other European cities. There are cafés and restaurants (though retailing in general is underdeveloped). There appears to be an adequate supply of food. A good proportion of people in the city centre – especially young people – are fashionably dressed. Although old-style cars predominate, there are a few second-hand western models and a conspicuous number of expensive imported vehicles such as generally large Mercedes saloons and Chrysler Jeeps.

These first impressions modify as one proceeds from the city centre through the suburbs. Buildings become less impressive and the imposing apartments of the centre give way to large and poorly finished blocks of flats. The people appear more shabbily dressed. 'New' restaurants compete jowl-by-jowl with establishments redolent of the Soviet era.

The deterioration continues as one leaves the city. Settlements in the country give the impression of having developed without design. The road through the village may be asphalt but side roads are just dirt tracks, cows amble along the streets and on the whole the level of amenities is low.

One of the subsequent aims of the project became the intention of capturing this diversity and these nuances as they affected firms and individuals.

METHODOLOGY

The research would have proved incredibly difficult had it not been for the considerable support given to us by a number of key individuals. They generously answered our many questions, facilitated additional contacts, opened what might have proved to be inaccessible doors. Whatever methodology we might have designed, it would have been very difficult to put into practice without the support of these individuals.

Our main method of collecting data has been to conduct semi-structured interviews with senior managers, middle managers, entrepreneurs and elected members and officers of the city and oblast administrations. These interviews were supplemented by innumerable informal conversations and discussions – in fact, we seized every opportunity to discover what people of all kinds thought of the current situation and the changes which they had experienced and were continuing to experience.

Data were also amassed through a process of observation of buildings, people, graffiti and other factors. We noticed closed-down factories in which some form of economic activity was still taking place, we noticed the diverse forms of economic activity, the evolving 'markets' which had replaced the centrally managed system of supply, we noted prices of goods and services and the persisting illogicalities of the former system (for example, householders continue to pay a flat rate for domestic gas, irrespective of volume of consumption, whereas electricity is metered).

A third source of data was the official publications and documents of the city and oblast administrations. The duma information centre proved an invaluable resource with up-to-date statistical and other information. We were also fortunate to be given a view of internal documents on the local economy.

A fourth source of data was the Russian press, both national and local. From being a mouthpiece of the communist regime, the press has developed into a varied and very active organism. Investigative journalism has grown apace and the press provides in-depth coverage of significant economic and political issues. Publications which we found to be particularly informative included the national publications *Argumenty i Fakty*, which also contains a regional supplement; *Ekonomist* which focuses on the regions; and *Izvestia*. At the local level *Deloviye Vesti*, *Inter* and *Volgogradskaja Pravda* provided useful sources of relevant information.

All these data sources we treated with considerable circumspection, using to as great a degree as possible multiple sources of data in order to check and verify what we discovered and what we were told. We were particularly cautious with statistical data, for the unreliability of statistics under the former regime is well known. We also heeded Birman's (1996) strictures regarding the limited reliability of contemporary Russian statistics and the incentives for misrepresentation (for example, the under-reporting of economic activity by both individuals and firms in order to maximize personal benefits).

We were particularly interested in statistics which indicated developments and portrayed trends, for while the data for particular points in time might be suspect, misreporting positive developments and playing down aspects of deterioration and decline (for instance, in the social sphere), we were hopeful that it would be extremely difficult to disguise the nature of developments in areas such as employment and health.

A further aspect of our methodology was to devise an analytical structure which would assist us in interpreting the data we had collected. The analysis was conducted at a number of levels.

First, we wanted to locate the investigation of firms and their managers in the context of the historical origins of the current situation. We therefore felt it necessary to outline the historical antecedents of the present, paying particular attention to the impact of Mikhail Gorbachev's perestroika and subsequent developments under Boris Yeltsin.

Second, we felt it necessary to achieve an understanding of the wider political and social context in which firms are currently operating as the survival and well-being of firms and individuals as components of social organization are inextricably linked. Third, we required a framework to analyse the situation and behaviour of different types of firm. Whilst all firms operated within Volgograd and its oblast, it was probable that the responses to the situation would be diverse, reflecting a range of factors. The typology of firms we developed is as follows:

- Old industrial enterprises: these represent the industrial dinosaurs of the Soviet system which had regarded them as its flagships. These enterprises were involved in processing raw materials and/or manufacturing capital equipment and components. In the past they had employed very large numbers of workers. In Volgograd these old industrial enterprises included the Red October Steel Plant, the Aluminium Plant, the Tractor Plant and the Parts Plant.

- The military enterprises: these enterprises were generally involved in high-technology production for military purposes and the space programme, although they did not necessarily concentrate exclusively on these activities. The employees of these military enterprises tended to comprise many highly qualified specialists and scientists. The collapse of the Soviet Union and the end of the Cold War have dealt a serious blow to this type of enterprise. Volgograd has a number of such military enterprises, including Avrora and Barrikady.

- Consumer-based enterprises: these tended to be the neglected step-children of the former system, producing consumer goods for everyday consumption, e.g. flour and milk products as well as furniture and motor cars. Many of these enterprises were related to the agricultural sector and in Volgograd were represented by firms such as the Meat Factory, Milk Factories No. 1, No. 2 and No. 3 and furniture factories.

- New small businesses: these businesses had been established as a result of economic changes of the latter part of the 1980s. Before this small private enterprise had been strictly regulated. These new businesses cover a wide range of activities in retailing, financial services and other services such as public transport (taxis). Many such businesses are small, transitory and in some cases unlicensed. Some are the result of the privatization of existing operating units (e.g. retail outlets), while others are truly new creations responding to the demands of a developing market economy.

- Criminal organizations: it is widely recognized that criminal organizations are active in a number of 'traditional' activities such as prostitution, gambling and 'protection'. The uncertainties of the change of system and the collapse of the former structure of authority have also provided opportunities for criminal activity in other areas such as raw materials and finance. The local press in Volgograd has frequently reported the existence of such activities.

The interviews were conducted with representatives of the first four types of firm, old industrial enterprises, military enterprises, consumer-based enterprises and new small businesses, that is with firms operating legally, although criminal activity was considered as a significant factor of the general environment in which business activity is carried out. However, before presenting the findings from the company interviews, the next two chapters set the scene of the provincial and regional context and the recent historical background.

2 The Povolzhsky Region

Volgograd and its oblast are a constituent of the Povolzhsky economic region, one of Russia's 11 economic regions. According to the Constitution of the Russian Federation the main aim of regional policy is to preserve the unity and integrity of the country and to prevent its disintegration into separate sovereign territories. The way to maintain this situation is seen to be in ensuring a balance between all-Russian interests and the interests of the individual regions. The other 10 economic regions are: North, North-West, Central, Central-Chernozem, Volgo-Viatsky, North-Caucasian, Urals, West-Siberian, East-Siberian and Far East economic regions. In its turn each economic region has its own constituent entities: oblasts and republics. The 11 economic regions encompass all 89 oblasts and republics of the Russian Federation.

The Povolzhsky economic region consists of six oblasts and two republics. These constituent entities are the oblasts of Uljianovsk, Saratov, Samara, Astrakhan, Voronezh and Volgograd as well as the republics of Tatarstan and Kalmykia. The oblast as an economic unit is considered to be an integral part of the Russian economy, however, with its own industrial specialization and internal economic ties.

The major principles on which the oblasts and republics are based are the following: economic principles, which consider the area as a specialized part of the integral national-economic complex of the country; nationality principle, which takes into account the ethnic composition of the population, particular characteristics of its labour force and modes of living; and administrative principles, which determine the units of economic organization and the territorial political–administrative arrangements. These principles are regarded as the major principles of the modern theory and practice of economic organization in Russia (Morozova, 1995).

We have chosen to describe the situation in the Povolzhsky economic region because of its importance in the overall Russian economy and to set the regional context for our investigation of transformation in Volgograd city and its oblast.

HISTORICAL AND GEOGRAPHICAL DATA

The Povolzhsky Economic Region (PER) holds third position among Russian's 11 economic regions from the viewpoint of its industrial potential, the development of agriculture, transport and science. Seven per cent of industrial and 14 per cent of agricultural production of the Russian Federation originate from this region. The territory of the PER covers 53,640 million hectares with a population of 16.9 million. The ethnic composition of the region, as in most of Russia, is very diverse. Approximately 70 per cent of the population consists of Russians. Other ethnic groups include Tatars, Kalmyks, Bashkirs, Chuvash and Kazakhs. There is still a large German community, which suffered greatly during Stalin's repressions, although many thousands have emigrated to Germany in recent years. The long-promised re-establishment of autonomy for the Volga Germans remains no more than a promise.

The geographical position of the region, with its access to major seas of European Russia such as the Caspian, White Sea, Baltic, Sea of Asov and Black Sea, has had a positive impact on the development of the region. However, the most important influence on the economy of the PER has been the River Volga – the main transportation artery for the European part of Russia. In fact the PER stretches from north to south along the 1500 kilometres of the Volga. Consequently, the major cities of the region are also major river ports. The region has more than 5700 km of internal waterways which are open for shipping for 250 days a year.

The history of the PER has well-established roots. The area became a part of the Muscovite state in the sixteenth century together with Kazan (capital of Tatarstan) and Astrakhan (capital of Astrakhan). In the same century between Kazan and Astrakhan, and approximately 300–400 km from each other, four castle-cities were built: Samara, Saratov, Astrakhan and Tsaritsyn (later Volgograd). Each of these cities is currently the capital of its respective oblast.

During the Second World War the regional economy was boosted by the numerous enterprises which were evacuated from the western part of the Soviet Union and relocated in the PER.

INDUSTRIAL STRUCTURE AND NATURAL RESOURCES

The major industries of the Povolzhsky region are oil and oil-refining, gas and chemicals. Until oil was discovered in Western Siberia the PER contained the largest discovered oil reserves in the former USSR. One of the greatest gas-producing complexes in Russia is also being constructed in the PER. In fact the largest Russian and global oil producer, LUKoil, has its origins here. According to industry experts the oil extracted in the region is of a high quality, which allows it to be used as an input for the chemical industry, with significant production of by-products such as paraffin (7–11 per cent), bitumen (12–20 per cent), light hydrocarbons and sulphur (3–3.5 per cent). The major oil extraction sites are situated in Tatarstan and Samara, Volgograd and Saratov oblasts. The Volgograd oblast oil refinery is the largest in the whole country. The region is also one of the major producers of synthetic rubber, industrial spirits, synthetic resins and plastics.

In the production structure of the Povolzhsky region the leading role is played by the machine-building complex, which includes tractors, cars, ships and aeroplane construction. The Volzhsky car factory in the city of Togliatti is renowned for the production of Lada cars. The production of construction materials, especially cement, is also well developed. The production of electricity utilizing the region's water resources is one of the major strengths of the region. There are several major electric power stations such as the Volzskaja power station (still named after Lenin), another Volzskaja power station (still named after the XXII Congress of the Communist Party of the Soviet Union) as well as the Saratovskaja and Nizhnekamenskaja power stations. The regional production of electrical energy per capita is one and a half times higher than the overall Russian average and accounts for approximately 10 per cent of all electrical energy produced in the country.

Agriculture is also one of the main specialisms of the region. From the viewpoint of lands cultivated for agriculture the region with its 8.7 million hectares is in third place in Russia after Altaij and Orenburg oblasts. Grain, sunflower seeds, corn, mustard, vegetables and the region's pride – water melons (which are claimed to be among the sweetest and biggest in Russia) – are cultivated here. The region is one of the greatest suppliers of meat and wool in Russia. The Volgograd region is also the major supplier of the delicious Russian black caviar and sturgeons to the domestic market and abroad.

The region's potential in natural resources is rich and varied. There are vast resources of mineral ore, shale, sodium chloride, sulphur and various components of building materials.

The relatively developed transport network allows the region to have extensive links with other regions of Russia and abroad. In fact all means of transportation are represented, such as rail, river, sea, air, motor and pipelines. Comparing the level of development of transportation with the rest of Russia, the PER has 2.5 times more railway lines, 6.5 times more pipelines, 1.7 times more river routes and 1.7 times more roads. In fact five out of the six railway lines that run through the country from west to east cross the region. There are also nine major airports with custom zones set up to facilitate export–import activities. The region exports oil, oil products, gas, electric energy, cement, tractors, motor cars, aeroplanes, machine tools and machinery, fish, corn, vegetables and water melons. Conversely it imports timber, mineral fertilizers, machinery and equipment, and textile and footwear products.

The economic development of the region is quite diverse. Side by side with highly developed territories such as Tatarstan and Volgograd, Saratov and Samara oblasts there is very little industrial development in the Republic of Kalmykia, which has a population density of just four people per square kilometre. The diversity of the economic situation in the Povolzhsky region can be illustrated by Table 2.1.

Table 2.1   Economic indicators in Povolzhsky region

Oblast	GDP per capita (million roubles)	Unemployment (%)	Minimum monthly income (thousand roubles)	Monthly average wages (thousand roubles)
Astrakhan	5.77	5.58	303.8	638.0
Volgograd	11.39	3.25	320.0	675.0
Voronezh	9.12	2.75	271.6	507.2
Samara	16.31	3.43	355.6	891.0
Saratov	8.36	3.70	340.5	495.2
Uljianovsk	6.82	3.27	212.0	523.7
Kalmykia	4.40	11.45	312.0	415.9
Tatarstan	14.57	2.12	256.6	733.4

Source: Based on *Delovoye Povolzhie*, no. 21 (1997), p. 3.

The most advanced entities of the region are Tatarstan and Samara, the middle group is formed by Volgograd and Voronezh oblasts, while the poorest are Kalmykia, Astrakhan, Saratov and Uljianovsk. On the regional scale it looks as if the situation deteriorates as one goes further South.

The Povolzhsky region is also an important part of the Russian military industrial complex. Volgograd and Samara oblasts are among the most militarized oblasts in the region. The latter has hundreds of enterprises producing for the defence industry and employing directly more that 200,000 people (or 40 per cent of the industrial labour force).

VOLGOGRAD AND VOLGOGRAD OBLAST

Volgograd oblast is the largest in the Volga River region and covers 114,000 km². The oblast consists of 33 administrative districts and six industrial cities containing over 2.7 million people; 1.2 million people live in Volgograd, the capital city of Volgograd oblast. It is situated approximately 1000 km south-east of Moscow and is probably the longest city in Russia, stretching for almost 100 km in a north–south direction on the right (western) bank of the Volga River. The width of the city (east to west) is often no more than 5 km.

The city of Volgograd was founded in 1589 as a frontier fortress to guard the Volga River. The city was originally named Tsaritsyn. It was the scene of a significant military action in the Civil War in which Stalin played an important role. Subsequently in April 1925 it was renamed Stalingrad, and with the adoption of the 1936 Constitution the oblast became Stalingradskaja oblast. In the West the city is known for its military significance in the Second World War. The Battle of Stalingrad, which lasted from 1942 to 1943, greatly influenced the outcome of the war. The Soviet victory concluding this epic battle halted the Nazi armies' eastward advance and precipitated the eventual collapse of the Third Reich. The battle is commemorated in a gigantic memorial comprising a towering sculpture to the Motherland.

On 10 November 1961 the then new General Secretary of the Soviet Communist Party, Nikita Khrushchev, the first Soviet official to denounce Stalin's crimes, changed the name of the city to Volgograd.

GEOGRAPHICAL AND ECONOMIC BACKGROUND

Volgograd oblast is surrounded by the economically developed oblasts of Saratov, Voronezh and Rostov and the relatively weak areas of Kalmykia and Astrakhan, as well as the Guriev region of Kazakhstan. The geographical location of Volgograd oblast offers many advantages. It is situated near the junction of the Volga and Don Rivers, which are the largest waterways in European Russia. Volgograd is connected to Western Russia, the Urals, the Caucasus and Kazakhstan by the Volga River and associated waterways. Major roads, air routes and waterways pass through the region and connect it to the rest of Russia, the Commonwealth Countries of the former USSR and the rest of the world. The annual turnover of all means of transport amounts to 17 billion tons/km with a passenger turnover of 4800 million passengers/km.

As previously mentioned, Volgograd is also a port with access to five different seas. The river and the canals are deep enough to accommodate the passage of cargo ships up to 5000 tons. The navigation period lasts from mid-April to late October. There are two waterside cargo terminals servicing Volgograd oblast, which can accommodate up to 22 loading and unloading ships per day.

There is also an international airport in Volgograd which has connections to 70 Russian cities and 10 cities abroad. There are regular connections to the German cities of Düsseldorf, Frankfurt am Main and Hanover.

In the Volga region, Volgograd ranks third in industrial output and is among the top industrial areas of Russia. Key areas of industrial activities comprise ferrous metallurgy, machine-building and chemical, petrochemical and fuel industries.

The major natural resource of the oblast is agricultural land, which covers 82 per cent of its area. The oblast's total volume of agricultural output ranks third in the Volga region; it ranks second for grain production. Over 8.2 million hectares of farmland yielding wheat, cotton, vegetables, various fruits and mustard crops make the area ninth in Russia in overall agricultural production. The farmers in the area also breed beef cattle, and sheep for wool and meat. This production is achieved in an area the climate of which is sharply continental. Summers are very dry and hot. It is not unusual to have + 30°C during July nights and + 43°C during the day. Winters are very cold with temperatures fluctuating between − 10°C and − 38°C.

The province is rich in natural resources. Oil and natural gas, phosphorites, cooking and chlormagnesium (bischofites) salts, mineral water, mason's sand, and limestone are abundant. The economic structure of the region based on total industrial output is illustrated by Table 2.2.

Table 2.2   Industrial output of Volgograd oblast

Branch	Percentage of total
Industrial production	43
Agriculture	16
Electric energy	17
Construction	12
Transport	15
Communication	4
Trade	14

Source: Based on Goskomstat (1997) p. 5.

Volgograd oblast is one of Russia's largest industrial centres with 438 large industrial enterprises, 627 agricultural enterprises, 11,808 farms and 2626 civil construction companies. As a result of its industrial output, Volgograd oblast occupies sixteenth position among the 89 similar areas. Volgograd's diversified industrial base includes machine-building (30 per cent), chemical and petrochemical industries (14 per cent), food processing (12 per cent), ferrous metallurgy (10 per cent), and light manufacturing (10 per cent).

Among the largest industrial enterprises in Volgograd oblast are the Red October Metallurgical Plant, the Volgograd Tractor Plant, the Volgograd Pipe Plant, Barrikady, the Aluminium Plant, the Volgograd Shipbuilding Plant and LUKoil Refinery. Other major industrial centres in the oblast include petrochemical/chemical plants, tyre manufacturing facilities and the pipe factory in Volzhsky (a satellite city, located 40 minutes from Volgograd city centre), the concrete factory in Michailovka and the textile plant in Kamyshin, one of the largest cotton processors in European Russia (ABC, 1997).

ECONOMIC SITUATION IN VOLGOGRAD OBLAST

Volgograd oblast was hit hard by the economic transformation. There was an avalanche-like fall in production of all branches of industry, with the exception of the fuel industry. Between 1990 and 1996 machine-building went down in volume terms by 81 per cent and ferrous metallurgy shrank by 82 per cent. In 1990 machine-building had represented 33 per cent and ferrous metallurgy 11 per cent of industrial production; by 1996 these industries represented only 14 and 7 per cent respectively. The production of rolled metal in 1996 decreased 13 times compared to 1990, of steel pipes 8 times. In 1996 production of tractors was only one-fifteenth of production in 1990, for synthetic rubber it was only one-twentieth.

The annual drop in industrial production in the oblast in 1996 was 10 per cent, compared to the Russian average of 5 per cent. In 1997 36 per cent of enterprises in the oblast were loss-making. On average the enterprises in the oblast were using only 42 per cent of their capacities. The complete closure of the enormous Red October Steel Works in Volgograd, which had formerly employed more than 30,000 people, was both fact and symbol of the critical stage in which the Volgograd area found itself during the reform years.

Part of the problems are on the demand side, in particular the collapse of the former USSR and COMECON markets, together with a sharp fall in overall national production. In part problems arise on the supply side and derive from sharp increases in energy prices. According to a report prepared by the Volgograd oblast administration the major problems are: mutual indebtedness of enterprises, lack of working capital and lack of demand, investments and opportunities for obtaining credits.

The major debtors in the region, with individual debts of more than 2 billion roubles, are Red October (269.6 billion), Volgograd Energo (265.9 billion), Volgograd Tractor Factory (96.4 billion), Barrikady (86.2 billion) and Volgogradnephtmash (78.2 billion). At the same time the federal budget is in debt to these and other enterprises to a total of some 475.15 million roubles.

The regional defence sector has been hit particularly hard by the transformation process. The catastrophic reduction in state orders and absence of federal budget finances for conversion have created a situation in which military production in 1997 had dived by 81 per cent compared to 1991. According to some estimates, in order to prevent closure of military enterprises, 350 billion roubles of investment are needed. However, the current state orders amount to only 50 per cent compared to 1990. The problem is aggravated also by the fact that the Ministry of Defence does not pay even for its own orders, and is among the major debtors to the locality.

THE AGRICULTURAL SECTOR

The agricultural sector has experienced all the negative consequences of the transformation. In 1996 agricultural production in the oblast had decreased by 43 per cent compared to 1990. The decline in the production of food-processing industries was even higher – 57 per cent. In the oblast there was a sharp decline in the usage of organic and mineral fertilizers, which had a further adverse effect on the productivity of land.

The sharply continental climate with hot dry summers requires use of irrigation systems. A catastrophic lack of finances does not allow the proper maintenance of existing systems and the development of new ones. The ambitious programmes which had been adopted at the end of the 1980s, and which were supposed to double the amount of irrigated land, have been completely abandoned.

During the past 5 years total livestock numbers have decreased by 43 per cent, including cattle (–22 per cent), pigs (–50 per cent) and sheep and goats (–58 per cent). Milk production decreased compared to 1990 by 29 per cent. The poultry population also shrank by 30 per cent. This process affected not only formerly state-owned kolchozes, but individual farms. In 1997 alone the livestock of individual farms in the oblast decreased by 17 per cent, including cattle (14 per cent), pigs (11 per cent) and sheep and goats (18 per cent).

Together with the drastic decrease in agricultural production was a growing share of imports. The dire situation in regional agriculture was exploited by international dealers in agricultural production. The market was filled with Western products. The weakness of the rouble, together with pauperization of the population, forced the dealers to buy extremely poor-quality, but better packaged cheap products. The situation was immediately seized upon by the opponents of the integration of Russia into the global trading system, who argued that imported third-class products represented the best which the West could offer Russia. In September 1997 even Yeltsin addressed the nation, urging them to ignore Western food products on account of their poor quality, and to buy good Russian ones.

Catastrophic increases in prices for agricultural machinery do not allow even the strongest collective farms, to say nothing of smaller agricultural producers, to purchase the equipment they require. During the past 5 years the volume of tractors and grain and forage combines decreased by 25–27 per cent. The existing machinery is becoming old and unreliable. Approximately 40 per cent of the agricultural machinery still in use is physically obsolete. According to the Deputy Chairman of Volgograd oblast's Committee on Economics and Finances the equipment which farms manage to obtain through leasing meets only approximately 10–12 per cent of their actual needs.

Among positive factors is the fact that the ownership structure in agriculture has completely changed. In 1989 98 per cent of the property in Volgograd oblast's agriculture belonged to the state in the form of kolchozes and sovhozes. Now more that 90 per cent of agricultural products are produced on private plots or on plots with mixed forms of ownership. At the end of 1997 there were 13,500 individual farms.

However, the changes in ownership in agriculture resemble changes in the ownership of industry, where often there are only formal changes which do not bring any fresh capital or personal commitment from the new owners. Not surprisingly, 75 per cent of all farms make heavy losses. The average monthly farm income at the end of 1997 was just 225,000 roubles (about $40), which is half that in industry (Bulatov, A., 'Zemelnye otnoshenia v rynochnoj ekonomike', *Ekonomist*, November 1997, p. 73).

In agriculture the problems with ownership are even more acute than in industry. The major question – sale of land to private individuals – had not been resolved at the time of writing. The Russian parliament, the Duma, with its strong communist representation, had several times blocked the presidential proposal to start the process of land privatization. The main arguments against land privatization are that the foreigners will buy Russia out, or 'new Russians' will purchase the most attractive plots of land, ruining agriculture already damaged by the demolition of the system of state collective farms. In fact it does not appear to be serious to talk about privatization in agriculture without privatization of land. The situation is paradoxical: the farmers who have use of the land of dismantled collective farms cannot have full control over it.

In February 1998 the Governor of Saratov oblast in the PER decided to go ahead without waiting for the Duma to adopt the necessary legislation. The sale of land was based on the principle of the highest bidder. The auction was so successful that the expected revenue from the sale was three times more than anticipated. However, this action was sharply criticized by members of the Volgograd Duma. One Volgograd MP even suggested that the Saratov Governor should be executed as a traitor to the Motherland. Considering the communist stranglehold in the Volgograd Duma, together with the oblast's communist governor, radical steps such as privatization of land will happen only if approved by the federal authorities.

The major problem which has to be resolved is that working on the land has to become profitable for farmers. However, under the current system of taxation approximately 70–75 per cent of revenue is taken in different kinds of taxes.

SOCIAL AND DEMOGRAPHIC ISSUES

According to the latest demographic survey of 1 January 1997 the population of Volgograd oblast was just over 2.7 million. The population in the oblast is more urbanized than the Russian average (78 per cent against 73 per cent). Almost half of the area's population live in two cities, Volgograd and its satellite city of Volzhsky (less than 10 km from the oblast capital).

There are 845,000 households in the area. The majority of households (36 per cent) consists of just two individuals. The average household comprises 3.2 persons. The economic upheavals could not but severely affect the demographic situation in the region. The birth rates are the lowest since the Second World War and are continuing to fall. In the period from 1990 to 1996 the number of registered marriages declined by 16 per cent. At the same time the divorce rate has increased by 18 per cent. The majority of Volgograd oblast families (46 per cent) has one child. Approximately one-third of families experience a divorce after less than 5 years of marriage.

Since 1992, for the first time since the Second World War, the population is declining. The decline is largely the result of an excess of deaths over births. In 1990 the birth rate per 1000 population was 13, but by 1995 the birth rate fell to 9.1 per 1000. In 1996 the difference between births and deaths was more than 17,000 people, compared with 3400 in 1992 (Goskomstat, 1996:3 and 28) (Table 2.3).

Table 2.3 The dynamics of population changes in Volgograd oblast (in thousands)

	1991	1993	1994	1995
Births	31.5	25.5	25.6	24.5
Deaths	30.8	36.9	41.4	39.6
Balance	+ 0.7	−11.4	−15.8	−15.1

Source: Dubova (1997) p. 115.

The situation, however, was partly offset by an inflow of new migrants from the military conflict zones and regions experiencing conflicts over nationality issues. In 1995 there were 24,300 migrants; however, the inflow of migrants seems to have reached its peak and is now going down; immigration will not be able to compensate, however, for the overall decline in the area's population.

LABOUR FORCE

The quality of the official labour, wages and income data is extremely poor. The economically active population in Volgograd oblast was 1.5 million, or 40 per cent of the total population. The official level of unemployment is 2.7 per cent (against 1.62 per cent in 1996), which is similar to the official Federal Russian unemployment figure. In December 1997 the area's unemployment offices had 36,700 registered unemployed. This represented an increase of 80 per cent compared to 1995. However, according to the Deputy of the Committee of Economics and Finances at the Volgograd oblast Administration the actual unemployment figure is approximately four to five times higher than the official one and total unemployment is considered to be 140,700, or more than 9 per cent of the active population.

The major decrease in work places is occurring in the major branches of the economy. In 1996 compared to 1995 the overall decrease was 4.1 per cent, with agricultural employment declining by 8.8 per cent and employment in construction by 9.3 per cent. At the same time there is a 5 per cent growth in the service sector of the economy. The employment in the state sector is rapidly falling, with a corresponding increase in employment in non-state sectors of the oblast economy (Table 2.4). The decline in production is occurring

Table 2.4   Sectoral structure of employment in Volgograd oblast

	1992	1993	1994	1996
Total employment	100	100	100	100
State sector	71	43	35	33
Non-state sector	29	57	65	67

Source: Dubova (1997) p. 115.

much faster than the increase in unemployment. Enterprises prefer to keep their labour force, on a basis of 1–3 working days a week. There is an obvious increase in this kind of employment, from 41.3 per cent in 1993 to 65.2 per cent in 1996. One of the alarming facts is that the period of time without employment is steadily growing. In 1995 11 per cent of the unemployed had been out of work for 1 year; in 1996 the figure had increased to almost 20 per cent (Dubova, 1997:117). Another new problem which needs addressing is the rapidly growing unemployment among school and university leavers. According to the Volgograd oblast statistics 70 per cent of graduates cannot find a job.

PERSONAL INCOME

The official minimum personal income level for 1996 was 329,000 roubles (about US$60). The number of people living below the official poverty line has increased steadily since 1991, and in 1996 half of the area's population had incomes which were lower than the official minimum.

The economic polarization of the oblast's population was also growing steadily. A measure of the inequality of income distribution is the Gini coefficient; the higher this is, the greater the inequality; in August 1996 it was 0.529. For comparison the Gini coefficient in the UK in 1979 was 0.30. The number of well-to-do people has been growing but so has the number of people on low incomes. In 1997 10 per cent of the wealthiest people in Volgograd oblast held 40 per cent of all personal incomes (23 per cent in 1995). However, the 10 per cent on the lowest incomes held only 1 per cent (3 per cent in 1995).

According to the local Goskomstat figures the monthly income of families with three or more children ranged between 38 and 54 per cent of the official minimum. For families with one or two children the same indicator was 99 and 79 per cent, respectively. Government income support programmes cannot even partly resolve this problem, as on average they supplement only about 20–25 per cent of the minimum income. The most acute problem, however, is the irregularity with which wages are paid. In 1997 two-thirds of all the oblast's enterprises and public-sector institutions had not paid salaries to their employees for more than 3 months.

HEALTH ISSUES

The collapse of the former health-care system in Russia, which was a result of the deteriorating general economic situation and severe budgetary problems, has had major negative effects on the local system of medical care. Following transformation, a majority of hospitals found themselves having only one-third of their 1991 budgets. The situation has resulted in serious difficulties. For example, the situation relating to AIDS in the area is far more serious than is generally the case in Russia. In 1989 the children's hospital was infected because of an absence of disposable syringes. Half of the infected children have already died. Since 1987 81 people have been identified in the area as HIV-positive, including eight foreign students. There are 12 HIV laboratories in the area; however, their level of medical equipment is extremely basic. The growth of illnesses with a so-called socioeconomic background is almost epidemic. In fact, the incidence of venereal diseases has increased 30 times during the last 5 years (*Ekonomist*, no. 1, 1998, p. 12). According to the director of the Institute for Socio-economic Problems of the Russian Academy of Science, 70 per cent of the population lives in a state of constant psychological and emotional stress (*ibid.*).

THE DEVELOPMENT OF MARKET INSTITUTIONS IN VOLGOGRAD OBLAST

Privatization

Since the launch of economic reform over 250 large, previously state-owned enterprises have been privatized under the Volgograd oblast auction system. Privatization of the formerly state-owned enterprises started in Volgograd oblast, as throughout Russia, in 1992 after the Privatization Law and the State programme of privatization in the Russian Federation were adopted.

The whole privatization process in the region is being executed by two bodies: the Committee for Property Management and the Property Fund. The former committee prepares enterprises for privatization, creates norms and makes decisions on privatization. The Property Fund is the actual seller of all the former state property. The system of privatization has separate mechanisms for the privatization of municipal enterprises and the privatization of regional and federal property.

Small-scale privatization

Small-scale (municipal) privatization involves the transfer of enterprises, that are targeted to be transferred into private hands (mostly these are the enterprises with balance-sheet value of up to 1 million roubles as of 1 July 1992 and with no more than 200 employees). Such enterprises include a range of stores and shops, enterprises in the service sphere, barbers' shops, cafés, etc.

Municipal privatization has been executed in two ways: sale of the whole enterprise through an open auction; and sale of the whole enterprise through commercial bidding (there is only one difference from open auctions – the bid winner has to fulfil certain conditions, so as to safeguard the nature of the enterprise, the number of personnel, etc.).

After a 3-year period of active municipal privatization more than 85 per cent of the social and cultural spheres of Volgograd's enterprises, about 90 per cent of the stores and more than half of the total number of enterprises, were transferred into the hands of new owners. The results of municipal privatization are obvious to anyone who is in a position to compare present-day Volgograd with Volgograd before the reform years.

Large-scale privatization

Large-scale privatization involves the privatization of medium and large enterprises (with a value over 1 million roubles and total personnel exceeding 200). Large-scale privatization is being executed mostly though the creation of joint-stock companies of open type from the assets of state enterprises. There are currently 470 joint-stock companies, 87 per cent of which are fully private, in Volgograd alone. Volgograd oblast occupies fifteenth place in Russia in terms of rates and results of privatization. There have been three main procedures for the sale of the shares of new-born joint-stock companies.

The First Option
A proportion of shares is sold for a nominal value (in some cases free of charge) to the enterprise employees. This process resulted in most of the privileges given to workers of enterprises being dictated not by economic expediency, but by political compromise with the industrial lobbies.

The Second Option
The system of privatization vouchers was introduced in order to involve wide groups of people in the privatization process. These privatization vouchers were given to every citizen of Russia, free of

charge, and had a nominal value of 10,000 roubles. A special guarantee certified the right of the voucher owner to a part of a previously state-owned company. The Volgogradians used their rights in the system of specialized Volgograd voucher auctions to secure ownership in companies. Such a system allowed anyone to become a shareholder of any enterprise regardless of location. At the end of 1994 there were more than 40 million such shareholders in Russia.

The Third Option
Obviously mass voucher privatization did not and could not solve the main financial problem of bringing real investment into enterprises. Collected privatization vouchers did not give anything of real value to the joint-stock companies. Investment bidding was intended to perform that function. Investment bidding is a method of selling the shares of joint-stock companies. The shares are offered in one package (15 per cent of charter capital and more) and are sold at the nominal value to the aspiring owner who proposes the best terms for the enterprise. This form of bidding did not become popular in Volgograd.

Small-business activity

More than 131,000 people, or 13 per cent of the total labour force, are involved in registered small-business activity, working in 13,000 enterprises. According to the authors' estimations at least as much as another half of that figure prefer not to register, in order to avoid paying any taxes. Every fourth Volgograd citizen is in one way or another connected with commercial activity. The area of small business, when viewed against the background of a sharp decline in industrial and agricultural production, looks very impressive. However, there are still many misunderstandings between these rapidly growing elements of a market economy and the old bureaucratic government practices. As the president of the Magnat corporation mentioned: 'Laws in the oblast are made in such a way that one cannot but break them all the time. In particular the region has such a system of taxation that to pay taxes in full not only will not allow you to earn anything, but will make you bankrupt right away' (*Deloviye vesti*, no. 8, December 1997, p. 3).

The problems which are confronting small business in the region are abundant, but according to the president of the Evko joint-stock company, 'Small business has to be protected not only from racketeers, but from corrupt state bureaucrats too' (*ibid.*).

In order to coordinate the business activity of small business with local government programmes a new local institution has been created. In December 1997 in Volgograd there was a conference which tried to bring entrepreneurs and the regional authority together. The conference has approved the creation of a municipal organization called 'Entrepreneurs of Volgograd oblast'. The first meeting of this group was scheduled for Spring 1998.

Securities market

As a result of privatization privatized enterprises became joint-stock companies. The securities market (i.e., the market for company shares) needs to be differentiated on two levels: primary market and secondary market. The primary market is where the initial sale of shares takes place. After this initial sale the shares may be traded in the secondary market – the market for already-existing shares.

The Primary Securities Market
The mass privatization of state enterprises on the basis of privatization vouchers began in Volgograd oblast in February 1993 and brought to the local securities market the shares of up to 10 new joint-stock companies every month. After most of the privatizations were completed this rate decreased to three or four companies per month. The primary sale of enterprise shares follows two main directions: (1) open sales for everyone; (2) sale of shares to the enterprise personnel according to the chosen option of privatization privileges.
   The open sales are executed in the following ways:

• sales through open auction (up to 43 per cent of shares have been sold in this way);

• sales through investment tenders (11 per cent);

• sales through specialized auctions (38 per cent);

• sales through commercial tenders (8 per cent).

Based on the number of participants, specialized auctions proved most popular: approximately 14 million persons and companies participated in these auctions. The figures for Volgograd oblast are as follows: 45 per cent of shares, that were on sale on the basis of privatization voucher auctions, were purchased by legal bodies, 12 per cent were purchased by specialized voucher foundations and 43 per cent were purchased by ordinary individuals.

The Secondary Market
These consist of two sectors in Volgograd oblast; these are the market of state responsibilities and the market of shares of privatized companies. According to research conducted by the American Business Centre in Volgograd these sectors are in practice not related, and are influenced by different groups of people. The market for bank shares, another important component of the securities market, is virtually absent. The shares of three local joint-stock banks are held by a small group of people who rarely exchange them.

There are estimated to be a couple of dozen intermediary firms which take an active part in secondary market selling and purchasing of shares. There are also three exchanges for security tenders: Volgograd Stock Exchange, the Fund Departments of Volgograd Universal Exchange and Nizhne-Volzhskaja Commodity Exchange. However, the monthly turnover of these exchanges is several times smaller than that of any of the intermediary firms. In fact, one of the main worries of Volgograd's mayor is the absence in the city of well-functioning, technically equipped stock and commodity exchanges: 'We cannot monitor the prices of securities in the city and because of that we just cannot be an active player there' (*Deloviye vesti*, no. 8. December 1997, p. 3).

ECONOMIC DEVELOPMENT ZONES

Volgograd is one of the leaders in this, for Russia, rather unusual incentive. The idea is to boost those enterprises, the shares of which are in the control of federal, regional or municipal authorities. In order to qualify to become an economic development zone another criterion besides state ownership is that the enterprise has to have workshops which have been closed for more than 12 months. The major benefit of being in the zone is that potential investors will enjoy a local tax holiday for at least 10 years.

To gain the status of 'zone of economic development' an enterprise has to provide a sound business plan and feasibility study which have to be approved by the city administration. At the moment several major, still-state-owned enterprises have applied for this status, including the Volgograd Tractor Plant, the closed Red October Plant and the former military enterprise Barrikady (*Deloviye vesti*, no. 8. December 1997, p. 2).

VOLGOGRAD'S CHAMBER OF COMMERCE

At the beginning of December 1997 the Volgograd Chamber of Commerce celebrated its seventh anniversary. In fact it had been established one year earlier than the Chamber of Commerce of the Russian Federation. The business activity of the chamber includes the major activities of institutions of this kind: marketing, information, provision of consulting and legal services and help in establishing contacts with foreign businesses.

The Volgograd Chamber has approximately 100 members, including private individuals as well as companies. Since 1993 the Chamber has been conducting so-called 'economic missions' to various countries. In 1997 alone there were three 'missions' to Austria, South Korea and Germany. Forty-five foreign companies, together with 250 local companies, took part in this activity and approximately 10 per cent of these companies signed contracts. The Chamber is also attempting to create a computerized data bank of potential business partners and to have an internet page, in cooperation with the well-known internet company 'Russia on line'.

The Chamber tries to raise companies' level of preparedness in looking for foreign investors, mainly through support in developing business plans. In fact, according to Chamber experts, none of more than 100 business plans prepared by local companies satisfies existing international standards. The problem which the Chamber is facing is that, parallel to teaching companies how to prepare business plans, it has itself to learn how to do them.

Together with Volgograd's Chamber of Commerce, another four of its branches have been opened in other districts of Volgograd oblast: Kamyshin, Michailovka, Zhirnovsk and Alekseevka. There are, however, no funds under the control of the Chamber; even the working capital helps only with stationery, although the potential of the Chamber is quite significant for the future development of the oblast.

The Chamber, parallel to its foreign activity, is now in charge of a 'Programme of Quality'. The programme aims to help local enterprises prepare themselves for achieving different international standards of quality such as ISO 9000, ISO 14000 and listing on Lloyds Register. In 1997 the Chamber received a grant of US$9000 from the USA-based International Centre of Entrepreneurship, which will allow the Chamber to establish a local centre for preparing managers for quality-control systems.

EXTERNAL TRADE RELATIONS

With the liberalization of international trade as a part of the reform package in 1991 Volgograd oblast started to develop its own pattern of independent export–import relations outside the control of the federal authorities. The abolition of the state monopoly on international trade relations substantially increased opportunities for those companies with some form of competitive advantage and severely handicapped those without. If in the past, during the centralized distribution of resources, inefficient companies could still enjoy the supply of foreign machinery and technology, now these companies must rely on themselves and on their own hard-currency earning potential.

Lack of an appropriate external trade infrastructure and expertise has made it hard for the oblast, especially during the first years of reform, to cope with organizing the export–import relations of the locality with the outside world. For instance, the concept of 'letter of credit' had to be introduced to the many bank managers via evening classes delivered by subcontracted practitioners from Moscow.

The problem was complicated even further because the meaning of the 'outside world' now also included the so-called 'near abroad', or former Soviet republics, which have introduced their own currencies, and Volgograd oblast lacked the administrative mechanism for external trade relations.

However, vast natural resources allowed the area in a very short time to overcome many of these problems. Absence of clear criteria, regulations, of what may be exported, how export should be controlled and monitored, together with often-corrupt customs officers, allowed entrepreneurial individuals and their companies to make fortunes during 1991–1993. Unregistered trains full of expensive raw materials were speedily transferred to the West and sold there.

Even when federal legislation on export–import relations started to appear, there were numerous loopholes allowing people in charge of production, distribution of natural resources or border customs to use and abuse the system. For example, when in 1992 some new restrictions were introduced on the export of aluminium from Russia, some of the regional entrepreneurs were still selling it in huge quantities – not as aluminium, but as simple spoons, for which there was suddenly a huge demand abroad. Needless to say, the spoons were made out of high-quality aluminium.

One way or another opportunities to earn big money through export–import in the area, together with Russian government concern about losses of the country's natural resources, created in a very short period of time quite an efficient external trade system backed by a new infrastructure (banking, information).

Since 1995 the external trade relations of the area have been characterized by a certain stability. According to the Volgograd Administration of External Trade Relations the much-needed stability can be explained by the fact that the bulk of the trade legislation has now been created, and people in Volgograd oblast operating in trade acquired some of the required knowledge. This is as true for Volgograd oblast as for its partners abroad (see Table 2.5).

Table 2.5   Regional export–import data

Main indicators ($million)	1995	1996	1997
Export	492.7	594.5	584.7
Import	271.4	182.3	209.8
Balance	221.3	412.2	374.9

Source: Based on internal data from Komitet Ekonomiki i Finansov Volgogradskoj oblasti (1998).

The positive balance can be explained by two major factors related to the structure of exports which are predominantly natural resource-based, and partly by the decline in the effective demand for imported goods due to the financial difficulties of the majority of the population of the oblast. However, the decrease in imports in 1996 compared with 1995 can also be explained by the fact that Western companies prefer to have their main dealers in Moscow or St Petersburg, with the result that foreign goods reach the area via internal routes.

The structure of exports is shown in Table 2.6. As one can see from the table the major export commodity (38.8 per cent of the total) is oil and oil-derived products; 65.3 per cent of all extracted petroleum

Table 2.6   The structure of exports

Product type ($m)	1995	1996
Oil and oil products	166.5	230.9
Chemical products	112.9	108.7
Ferrous and non-ferrous metals and related products	46.1	26.6
Raw aluminium	83.5	125.9
Machine-building products	10.2	29.9
Agricultural and food products	23.7	37.6

Source: Based on internal data from Komitet Ekonomiki i Finansov Volgogradskoj oblasti (1998).

is exported. Exports go mostly to Ireland, the Czech Republic, Slovakia, Italy, Germany and Liberia. The exports of chemical products and aluminium are substantial. Among the exports of the chemical industry 69 per cent are constituted by organic and inorganic chemicals.

The export of machinery and equipment represents just 5 per cent of total exports. Agricultural exports accounted for US$37.6 million or 6.3 per cent of exports. The major agricultural products exported were sunflower seeds, wheat, mustard seeds, milk and milk products.

Imports represented 31 per cent of total economic turnover. The major imports include chemical products such as ammonia, phenols, acids, vitamins and other pharmaceutical products. Twenty-seven per cent of total imports are accounted for by plant and equipment, coming mostly from the developed countries. Agricultural imports are not substantial, amounting to about 4 per cent of imports and consisting mostly of sugar, flour, grain, meat and meat products, vegetables and confectionery.

There is an expected negative balance between the import of services into the area and the export of services. Exports of services are valued at $3.9 million, with communications accounting for 52 per cent, transport services 28 per cent, engineering services 9 per cent, tourism 6 per cent and marketing and education 3 and 2 per cent respectively. The services of the area were utilized by 88 different countries with the majority of orders coming from Germany (11.6 per cent), Iran (11.3 per cent), Latvia (9.8 per cent), Finland (6 per cent), Greece (5.6 per cent) and Turkey (5.5 per cent). Services to the former Soviet republics accounted for 34.7 billion roubles. The major customers were the Ukraine, Kazakhstan, Uzbekistan and Moldova.

The import of services has been calculated at $21.9 million. Twenty-eight different countries provided these services; 57 per cent was represented by engineering services; construction accounted for 18 per cent and consultancy services for 17 per cent. The major service providers are Lebanon (17.4 per cent), Germany (14.6 per cent), Turkey (8.2 per cent), Canada (5.5 per cent) and the USA (1 per cent). The volume of imported services from the 'near abroad' amounted to 16.8 billion roubles and consisted mostly of transportation services from the Ukraine and Belorussia.

HARD CURRENCY INCOME

There were more than US$400 million in the bank accounts of enterprises in the oblast; 48.7 per cent were received from the export of goods, 0.6 per cent from the sale of services, financial credits provided a further 23.1 per cent and an equivalent amount was purchased on the internal currency market. The remaining 4.4 per cent represented earned interest and the sale of securities.

The fact that US$297.1 million (or 74.3 per cent) is concentrated in Volgograd with another US$99.9 million or 25 per cent in Volgograd's satellite, Volzhsky, signifies that virtually all international transactions go through only two cities in the oblast where the banking sector is relatively better developed than in the rest of the area.

As for expenditures during 1996, US$404.336 million have been spent on imports of industrial products (22.1 per cent) and on import of services (6.3 per cent); 16.9 per cent went to service debts, 41.6 per cent was sold on the internal currency market and other hard currency operations involved another 12.4 per cent.

Foreign direct investment

FDI was perceived in Russia as a panacea for the current investment crisis. Foreign investment has been widely regarded as a vitally important source of new technology and managerial know-how. FDI was supposed to provide much-needed access to Western capital markets and was considered critical for the restructuring of obsolete Russian industries. There was a strong belief that Russian companies would gain access to Western markets via FDI. It was also widely believed that FDI would help in the process of demonopolization, boosting competition, the development of the private sector and the creation of a new economic system.

The prevailing belief was that 'Foreign direct investment was an important catalyst for economic changes in transitional economies, offering host countries external resources, technology, management, and access to foreign markets' (OECD, 1993:7).

At the end of 1995 FDI in the Russian Federation had reached $2.8 billion. According to the Russian Ministry of the Economy, FDI flows reached $5 billion in 1996, $6 billion in 1997 and will increase to $10 billion per year by the end of the century.

One of the problems which regionally based companies face in attracting FDI is the lack of well-researched and well-prepared business plans with feasibility studies drawn up according to recognized Western requirements. The Lower Volga Fund, which was established with the help of the European Bank for Reconstruction and Development together with the American Business Centre with the purpose of helping companies in preparing the necessary documents for investors, assessed in the 2-year period of its existence more that 100 projects and declared them all to be unsatisfactory. None of these projects, understandably, was successful in attracting investment. The major worry of foreign investors is not so much political instability in Russia as the low level of management expertise in the enterprises.

PROBLEMS WITH FDI ESTIMATION

The existing estimates of FDI differ considerably from one source to another in terms of estimating the stock and flow of FDI. There are several reasons for this (Astapovich, 1995:29).

Firstly, the difference between *declared* (or committed) and *actual* flows of FDI. According to the Ministry of Finance, at the initial stages of investment only 10–15 per cent of declared investments were actually realized. According to Russian Foreign Investment Law (when it was adopted), foreign participants must invest no less than 50 per cent of the investment capital declared in the constituent documents, but the sanctions for not doing so are not well developed and are often ignored.

Secondly, according to existing Russian statistical practice, both declared and actual investments are considered 'foreign investment'. However, in the case of establishing joint ventures, both foreign and Russian partners invest capital. As a result, the share of foreign capital is smaller than the declared or actual investment. According to the state registration chamber, the percentage of foreign investment from March 1992 to January 1995 amounted to 57.5 per cent of the total value of investment of registered Russian–Foreign Joint ventures (RFJV).

Thirdly, very often RFJV tend to hide the information necessary for the assessment of the flow of FDI by government bodies such as Russian Federation Goskomstat, fearing disclosure of their investment activities to criminal organizations. This non-disclosure of information results in tax avoidance in some cases.

Fourthly, discrepancies result in statistical information due to the fact that there are five different organizations responsible for the registration of foreign investment, such as municipalities, district organizations, State Taxation Service and Customs Service.

Fifthly, the dispersion of exchange rates preconditions the difference in the valuation of particular cost indicators. High inflation in Russia and constantly changing hard-currency exchange rates make comparison quite difficult.

In 1997 there were 285 registered companies with foreign capital in the oblast. The total amount of invested capital amounted to 80 billion roubles or about US$16 million. Companies from 50 countries invested their capital in joint ventures. The majority of invested capital came from the US, Great Britain, Italy, Germany, Poland, the Ukraine and Turkey. The obvious difference between registered and

Table 2.7 Number of RFJV by branch of industry

	No. of registered RFJV		No. of actually functioning RFJV	
	1995	1996	1995	1996
Industry	49	53	30	30
Agriculture	6	6	4	4
Transport and communications	4	6	2	2
Trade and catering	117	125	69	59
General commerce	19	19	10	9
Geology	2	2	2	2
Science	7	7	2	2
Others	11	40	9	11
Total	**247**	**285**	**146**	**140**

Source: Based on internal data from Komitet Ekonomiki i Finansov (1997).

actually functioning joint ventures is quite striking. Only 50 per cent of all registered joint ventures are actually operating.

Table 2.8   The major indicators of RFJV activities

	1993	1994	1995	1996
Volume of production (billion roubles)	96.0	108.0	291.0	525.2
Employment	2954.0	2777.0	4086.0	4628.0
Wages fund (billion roubles)	3.2	7.1	24.7	61.7
Exports ($ million)	36.0	17.0	9.0	33.8
Imports ($ million)	18.0	17.0	18.0	56.3

Source: Based on internal data from Komitet Ekonomiki i Finansov (1997).

Some of the major projects with foreign partners are:

• oil exploration and mining with the participation of the French firm Elf-Aquitaine and the German firm Dominex;

• oil processing RFJV between Volgograd oblast and a British corporation;

• bishophite mining and processing involving Volgograd oblast and US companies;

• construction of a cardiological centre in conjunction with the Croatian firm Ingra and the German firm Hospital International;

• construction of a major bridge across the Volga River with the collaboration of the Greek company Etep and a British firm.

CONCLUSION

Since the beginning of the reforms the Povolzhsky region in general, and Volgograd oblast in particular, have experienced the tremendous impact of changes in the economic policy of the Russian Federal government. Overnight destruction of the institutions of the centrally planned economy left the oblast isolated from the traditional 'life-supporting mechanisms'. The majority of industries, budget institutions and agriculture were hit very hard. During the first 3 years after the introduction of the reform package of 1992 the general feeling among the majority of the population was that life was collapsing and there was nothing one could do about it. As one respondent, a democratically oriented professor at Volgograd University, said about 1994: 'We felt confused and betrayed. The democracy and the market economy we were fighting for turned out to be completely different from what we had expected. Turbulent times brought to the surface the worst of people and in people. Democracy and market economy showed up only their negative side to us. The first materialized in the opportunity for corrupt people who now could be elected and who now openly enjoyed criminally accumulated wealth. Freedom brought out fascist anti-Semitic and nationalistic movements openly on to the streets. The market hit us with its darkest weapons: huge inflation, insecurity, fall in all kinds of production. Capitalism showed us its ugly face without showing the expected benefits it could bring.'

However, in talking about 1998 the same professor was much more optimistic when describing the situation in the area: 'People have absorbed the shock of realization that there is no one but themselves who is responsible for their well-being. No state, no local party committee, no one but themselves. And people started to move, looking not at what they can do and constantly recalling what and who they were, but what they can offer to the market now, whether the market needs it. The same change in attitude is seen among the majority of the oblast institutions.'

3 Centre and Province: an Evolving Relationship

INTRODUCTION

The preceding chapter examined the economic structure of Volgograd oblast in the context of its regional setting. The current chapter explores the evolving political situation as power and authority are redefined and reallocated. The broad contours of the transition from communism are well known and have been well documented (e.g., Sakwa, 1996). Attempts to address the crisis of the communist system under Gorbachev, by introducing glasnost and perestroika, ultimately resulted in a chain of events including the demise of the communist system in the USSR and in Eastern Europe, the disintegration of the USSR itself and the decision to establish a political democracy and a market economy under Yeltsin. All in all these developments resulted in a movement of power and authority away from the centre. Previously power and authority had radiated from Moscow. The centre has since the reforms increasingly sought to delegate more competences to regional and provincial bodies while at the same time striving to safeguard the integrity of the Russian Federation. Clearly this process has not always run smoothly as the regional and provincial bodies have attempted to assert their positions, seizing as much power as possible to themselves, consequently becoming involved in conflicts with the centre and other more local 'competitors'.

It is this issue of federal, regional, provincial and municipal relations which this chapter now addresses. The chapter investigates the transition from communism to capitalism, with particular emphasis on the regional level and the related impact on companies. Power, formerly concentrated at the centre, is now partially delegated to the regional and provincial levels This delegation, however, is effective only to a certain degree. There is now not always clarity as to who is responsible for what. Instructions and resources trickle down slowly from the centre and sometimes do not even reach their destinations. The devolution of political power has also contributed to the consolidation of local power bases and the emergence (and transformation) of local élites. This development has also been characterized by frictions, for example, between city and province. This friction emanates in part from the unequal pace of developments in urban and rural areas. Often urban areas are more progressive and open to change, while the rural areas are more conservative and suspicious of the enormous changes which are taking place in Russia.

A further characteristic of the situation in the province (not in all provinces but in many including Volgograd) is the continuing influence of communists and the Communist Party. The nature of this communist influence can be quite variable (from traditional Leninist to what may be styled 'Euro-communist'). In Volgograd and its province there is still substantial communist influence but on the whole it presents itself as pragmatic rather than nostalgic; that is, it seeks to resolve the difficulties of the current situation rather than re-create the status quo existing before the reforms initiated by Gorbachev.

LAST STEPS TO DISINTEGRATION

The period under Mikhail Gorbachev's leadership occupies a special place in Soviet and post-Soviet history. The early 1980s were a period of stagnation and uncertainty. Following Leonid Brezhnev's death in November 1982, and the death of his successor, Konstantin Chernenko, in March 1985, Mikhail Sergeevich Gorbachev was elected General Secretary of the Communist Party of the Soviet Union (CPSU). Cardinal changes in the life of the country were expected to come with his appointment. In April 1985 a plenary meeting of the CPSU Central Committee was held, which declared the 'acceleration' (uskorenie) of the Soviet Union's socioeconomic development. The plenary session noted 'socialism's potential had been insufficiently used'.

The strategy of acceleration embraced the economic and social spheres as well as scientific–technological progress. The acceleration strategy, however, ran out of steam with glasnost (openness) and perestroika (restructuring). Glasnost uncovered the shortcomings of socialist developments and strengthened criticism and self-criticism in society in order to 'clean up the inheritance of the past'. Perestroika was meant to introduce structural and organizational changes in socialist society. Simultaneously perestroika was intended to democratize the whole of societal life and to widen the conditions facilitating the realization of people's potential and socioeconomic and spiritual needs.

In March 1986 the XXVII Congress of the CPSU was held, and adopted the new version of the Third Party Programme. The tasks laid down in the programme were ambitious. First of all the whole of the economic potential of the Soviet Union had to be doubled by the year 2000. Labour productivity was planned to rise 2.5 times. Each Soviet family was promised its own flat. During the Congress important pieces of legislation on leasing, cooperatives and joint ventures were adopted. In 1986 the new law on working collectives was adopted which laid the foundation for economic self-sufficiency of enterprises; in 1988 the revolutionary 'Law on private activities' sanctioned private enterpreneurship in 30 types of economic activity. By the year 1990 more than 7 million citizens, or 5 per cent of the working population, were working in the cooperative sector of the economy.

In 1989, during the XIX Communist Party Conference, the decision was made to create a state based on legal principles. So, after 70 years of the 'best democracy in the world' there came a realization that the law had to be the major coordinator of socioeconomic and political life and not arbitrary decisions of the Party's functionaries. Under pressure from Gorbachev it was decided to remove party organs from the economic management of the country at local level and strengthen the power of Soviets (or representative bodies).

In May 1989 the First Congress of People's Deputies was divided between those who were in favour of Gorbachev's reforms and those who wanted to go even further and totally destroy the existence of the unitary, barrack-like socialist state. The first camp was still using communist phraseology and was appealing to Lenin's legacy. However, the second group, led by Andrei Sacharov, Boris Yeltsin and Yuri Afanasiev, was insisting among other things on 'moving the economy on to market rails'.

In December 1989 the Second Congress of People's Deputies was held. Yeltsin showed himself to be an important leader and emphasized especially the necessity to struggle against bureaucracy and privileges. He was the initiator of a concept in which he himself probably believed that the reforms had to be introduced without worsening the living conditions of the ordinary people.

In March 1990 the Third Congress of People's Deputies adopted a historical decision: to revoke the 6th Chapter of the Constitution, which declared the CPSU to be the core of the political system of the USSR. All forms of party control at enterprises, in administrative organizations and the army had now to be abolished. At the Congress Gorbachev was elected as the first and (as history was to show less than 2 years later) the last President of the USSR; the market mechanism was also stipulated as the principal regulator of economic life.

The breathtaking developments in Soviet political life were, however, paralleled by a worsening of the economic situation of the country. The long-accumulated weaknesses of the Soviet economy became more and more apparent. Factories, plants and construction sites were ceasing to work. Gross domestic product (GDP) was steadily declining. Worsening economic conditions, together with the liberalization of the country's emigration policy, created an increasing brain drain. In 1991 alone 70,000 scientists and engineers emigrated to the US. According to the official statistics no more that 16 per cent of industrial production was able to match the competition from the West and 67 per cent of industrial equipment in the Soviet Union was in a critical state.

The problems of the 1980s were not just a temporary phenomenon due to the changes taking place in the economy and politics of the USSR; they were indicators of the deep and growing crisis of the entire administrative and command system. To escape these problems the policy of 'acceleration' was in itself not sufficient. Perestroika, of which the major slogan was 'more socialism', was failing to deliver the promised results.

The existing system based on Marxism was just not susceptible to reform. Gorbachev's belief that it was possible to improve the system by injecting more 'genuine' Marxism–Leninism was contradictory in nature as any presumed improvements would actually mean moving backwards and not forwards. Glasnost revealed the fundamental errors of the previous communist years and questioned the legitimacy of communist rule.

Economic problems, weakening of the political grip of the Communist Party, together with the realization of the need for radical transformation of the USSR, brought into question the very purpose of preserving the Soviet empire. The republics were putting pressure on the weakening centre for greater autonomy, whilst contemporaneously searching for their own identities. In 1988 the first warfare erupted between Armenia and Azerbaijan over Nagorno-Karabakh, an Azerbaijani territory with an Armenian majority. In 1990 pogroms of Armenians erupted in the capital of Azerbaijan, Baku. According to General Lebed, who was in charge of restoring law and order there, people were running for their lives from medieval cruelty, in an hour losing everything that was the essence of human life' (Lebed, 1995:242).

In the Baltic republics the movement to leave the USSR was gathering momentum. However, the referendum called by Gorbachev on 17 March 1991 showed that 71.3 per cent of the population of the Soviet Union were in favour of preserving the USSR. A new treaty which was supposed to combine the republics' desire for a greater independence and a much looser federation of Soviet republics was due to be signed on 21 August 1991. The failed coup of 19 August 1991, conducted by communist hard-liners to prevent the emergence of new federal relations within the USSR, actually quickened the process of disintegration. At the end of the year (8 December 1991) representatives of the Ukraine, Belorussia and Russia signed an agreement which created the Commonwealth of Independent States (CIS). This agreement stated that the USSR, as a subject of international law, ceased to exist, leaving 25 million Russians cut off from Russia in 14 newly established countries. The initial joy of reformers that Russia could speed up its political reforms, once freed of its empire, was sobered by the realization of the magnitude of the economic problems associated with the disintegration of the country and the psychological feeling of loss of its own Soviet Union identity.

PROVINCE VERSUS CENTRE

Since 1992, and especially during the local regional elections of 1996–7, the Russian Federation experienced a similar situation to the period when the Soviet Union under Gorbachev lost control over its republics. The regions and oblasts were strengthening their executive and legislative branches, their governments and their economic and financial structures.

Exploiting the weakness of the centre the federation's subjects increased their gold reserves, created their own monetary systems based on oblast and regional bonds, IOUs and promissory notes.

Some regions declared that they owned their natural resources and refused to pay federal taxes. The magnitude of the fiscal problem can be illustrated by the fact that in April 1997 Moscow's share of tax contributions to the federal budget was just slightly less than half, the rest of the taxes were shared between the remaining constituent bodies (republics and oblasts) of Russia (*Delovoye Povolzhie*, no. 27, 1997, p. 9).

Some commentators believe that the West is trying to encourage Russian's regions and oblasts in their centrifugal tendencies in order to facilitate the West's access to raw materials. Doing business directly with Russian regions, bypassing the federal authorities in Moscow, removes a substantial bureaucratic level, shortening the decision-making process. The West tries to influence the regions by encouraging them to adopt legislation which is necessary and favourable to Western companies. Western business no longer seems to consider the Russian centre as the best guarantor for its investment.

Some regions, with their own concepts of how best to attract foreign direct investment, are very successful. Probably the best example of this is Novgorod oblast in north-west Russia. The oblast has a well-developed package to attract investors, including tax-free zones, provision of guarantees based on the oblast's industrial resources and the personal guarantees of the members of the oblast administration. As a result the amount of FDI increased 44 times, from US$3.5 million in 1994 to US$1534 million in 1996. The same 'investment-friendly packages' are available in Samara oblast, Kaliningrad, Ekaterinburg, Novosibirsk and St Petersburg.

The hardship experienced by the majority of the population, and the deep dissatisfaction with the results of Moscow's economic policy, have created a strong opposition among some of the people living in Russia's regions and oblasts. The most consistent critics of the current economic policy come from the left, from the communist side of the political spectrum in Russia. No wonder that people vote for the communists. As an expression of dissatisfaction with the current government people elect both die-hard communists and some popular new Russian capitalists: in this way they combine both choice and Marxism–Leninism.

In 1996 in the majority of Russian oblasts there were elections for oblast gubernators (governors). In oblasts such as Magadan, Cheliabinsk, Briansk, Riazan, Kurgan, Krasnojarsk, Stavropol and Volgograd the posts of gubernator or his deputy were assumed by communists. These oblasts constitute the so-called 'Red Belt' of Russia. In most of these cases, in the Russian oblast parliament, the Duma, communists were also elected and represent a substantial proportion of deputies. In fact, and Volgograd oblast is a typical example of it, if a person wants to be elected to the Duma or be employed by the local government administration, it is useful to be a member of the Communist Party. Old habits die really hard. Communists are a blocking minority in the oblast Duma. In the city Duma out of its 24 members, 22 are communists. No wonder that they insist on being called not by the old Russian word 'Duma', but by the expression which is more common to their ears: 'Soviet of People's Deputies', the name used since the Russian Revolution. The word 'tovarischi' (comrades) is also widely used during Duma meetings.

Often the adoption of legislation depends on who made the initial proposal. If communist, then the chances of it being adopted are high; if the representative of another party or an independent member, then the opposite is true. The communists, following tradition, are very disciplined, vote as one body and as a rule attend all of the Duma's sessions.

The situation with communists in the majority creates a problem though. The 'Red' Duma with its gubernator has to manoeuvre between Moscow's 'capitalists', who are in charge of the current federal government, and the local electorate.

INTER-BUDGETARY RELATIONS IN THE RUSSIAN FEDERATION

According to Lavrov (1998) the existing system of inter-budgetary relations in Russia does not provide stimuli for regional and municipal authorities to conduct a responsible and economically sound budgetary policy. Republics and oblasts often threaten the Federal authorities by threatening not to pay Federal taxes to the Federal budget. In fact, four republics (Tatarstan, Bashkotorstan, Yakutia and Chechenia) already partially stopped fulfilling their obligations towards the central budget. There is a danger that if the economic and political situation in Russia worsens, 'the threat of budgetary separatism will appear again' (Lavrov, 1998).

The complicated relations between oblasts' budgets and the Federal budget is mostly due to the non-monetary instruments which are widely in use when settling fiscal relations between them. Non-monetary instruments used by regional and municipal budgets include: promissory notes, barter and mutual reconciliation of debts. The introduction of non-monetary payments to Federal and oblast budgets took place in 1994, when the Federal government, unable to meet its obligations to oblasts, started to use promissory notes, treasury tax relief and different forms of mutual cancellation of debts.

The enormous distortions which naturally have arisen from this kind of budgetary accountancy led to mutual accusations between oblasts and the Federation of either paying too little or paying too much.

At the end of 1997 the Federal government decided to stop non-monetary budget payments, but this was virtually ignored as oblasts realized the benefits of having this kind of system. In fact more and more oblasts are issuing their own promissory notes, ignoring the Federal Law on simple and transferable promissory notes of March 1997, which forbids the Federal subjects from using such instruments. According to the Ministry of Economics in 1996 on average 50 per cent of all fiscal payments into oblast and municipal budgets were made in non-monetary forms. According to Russian Treasury data of 1997 the mutual cancellation of debts amounted to 46 per cent of the value of all payments. The share of non-monetary payments amounted to 70–80 per cent of payments themselves.

Regional and municipal authorities are keen to widen the use of non-monetary payments. There are several reasons for this (Lavrov, 1998). Firstly, cancellation of debts is a hidden form of budgetary subsidy to enterprises, which allows the latter to preserve work places without any regard to efficiency. Cutting non-monetary payments in favour of monetary payments would put many enterprises at the end of bankruptcy which oblast administrations, whose members often have a personal interest in individual enterprises, cannot afford. Secondly, allowing or not allowing enterprises to use non-monetary payments is a powerful lever in the hands of oblast administrations over privatized and formally independent enterprises. Thirdly, to get non-monetary payments from enterprises is incomparably more easy than getting enterprises to pay with their limited cash. Fourthly, non-monetary payments allow oblasts to redistribute budgetary payments, reserving a larger share for themselves and transferring less to the Federal budget. According to current legislation, when paying taxes, enterprises have first to clear previous debts and then their current obligations. The debt to the Federal budget is generally larger than the debt to oblast budgets, which means that if enterprises were to pay their taxes with real money, most of the cash would pass to the Federal budget.

Widespread usage of non-monetary budgetary payments allows oblasts and municipal authorities to make ends meet. As a rule they do not have access to credits and limited non-tax income. However, the negative results of this system are quite obvious, from price distortions and the creation at enterprise level of strong expectations to retain the use of non-monetary forms of payments in the future to the absence of cash in oblast budgets which delays or prevents the payment of wages and social benefits.

OBLAST FINANCES

The oblast budget is regulated by the oblast 'Law on budget and budgetary process in Volgograd oblast', adopted in 1993. According to this law the budget system consists of two levels: oblast budget and the budgets of the municipalities. The oblast revenue also forms part of the Federal budget.

The revenue composition of the oblast budget, with the deductions to the Federal budget, is shown in Table 3.1. More than half of the tax revenues (51.2 per cent) go to the Federal budget, because the centre takes most indirect taxes while most of the direct taxes are collected at the oblast level. The oblast budget receives 69.1 per cent of the taxes on enterprise profits, 90 per cent of the income tax, 62.4 per cent of taxes for natural resources exploitation and almost all of the enterprise property tax.

Table 3.1 Tax assessment

Type of taxes	Federal budget (%)	Oblast budget (%)
Tax revenues	51.20	48.80
Including:		
On profit	30.90	69.10
VAT	78.30	21.70
Property tax	0.95	99.05
Tax on usage of natural resources	37.60	62.40
Tax on external trade operations	100.00	–
Others	2.20	97.80

Source: Sedov (1996) p. 28.

The centre, in spite of Yeltsin's promise to 'give them as much power as they can swallow', is concerned about losing its influence over the regions. Using the newly adopted Tax Code of the Russian Federation the centre tries to shift the taxes which are the most difficult to collect on to the regions. For example, the regions are empowered to collect 90 per cent of corporation tax, which depends totally on enterprise performance, and the property tax, which is extremely difficult to define in the absence of appropriate property and land legislation. However, the centre retains the easiest tax to collect, VAT at 22 per cent, for itself.

Interestingly, more and more of the oblast budget revenue comes from sources other than taxes. If in 1995 taxes constituted 90–4 per cent of the budget revenue, in 1997 the tax share fell to 54 per cent. This trend is explained by the commercialization of the social sphere. Taxpayers themselves are paying more and more for education, accommodation and health care. On the other hand, oblasts themselves are more heavily involved in commercial activity, especially exporting. Many oblasts also receive financial support from the Federal government.

Volgograd oblast, like the majority of the Russian provinces, is in deep financial crisis. At the beginning of 1997 the oblast budget deficit reached an astronomical 150 billion roubles. In 1997 the budget authorities failed to collect 20 per cent of taxes. According to the oblast General Prosecutor, 11,000 enterprises and entrepreneurs failed to register in the state tax office, with the aim of avoiding paying tax.

The debt to the budget of the 103 largest enterprises of the oblast constitutes more than half of the budget deficit. Among the most notorious non-payers of tax are the 'Red October' steel works, the Tractor Plant, Pipe Plant (Trubny zavod) and Barrikady (Ledin V., *Inter*, no. 27, 1997).

THE RELATIONSHIP BETWEEN OBLAST AND FEDERAL BUDGETS

Fifteen per cent of the tax revenues of the Federal budget are aimed at supporting the oblasts of Russia. In order to receive Federal financial support oblasts have to qualify for one out of two categories of support. The oblast has to have the status of 'oblast in need of support' or of 'oblast in substantial need of support'. The first status is granted if the average income per capita is lower than the Russian average. The second status is granted to oblasts in which the planned expenditure of the budget is lower than planned revenue. The Federal support fund is divided on the basis of these two statuses. For instance, in 1996 the proportions were: 65.79 per cent of the Fund to support 'the oblast in need' and 34.21 per cent of the Fund to support 'the oblast in substantial need'.

In 1996 Volgograd oblast was allocated from the Federal support funds transfers amounting to 390.4 billion roubles, but only 317.6 billion roubles (or 81 per cent of the money) were actually transferred. Federal programmes at the oblast level such as 'Children of Russia', 'Accommodation', 'Machine-building for the agricultural complex' and some others received only 47 per cent of the allocated funds. These facts do not add to the popularity of the centre's economic reforms nor personally of president Yeltsin, who has been sharply criticized by the oblast and Volgograd Dumas' MPs. The problem, according to some of the oblast MPs, is not only in the fact that the Federal budget experiences numerous problems, but that Moscow is irritated by the communist presence in Volgograd oblast and is trying to 'punish communists for the things they believe in'.

However, Moscow believes that the oblast finances would be much healthier if the oblast administration were tougher on persistent tax defaulters, such as the previously mentioned industrial giants. The latter enjoy 'special relations' with the oblast administration. In fact, the oblast administration is extremely protectionist and the Gubernator has a Council of Directors comprising 15 directors of leading companies, the majority of which are loss-making enterprises.

According to the oblast exchequer oblast finances are often misused. In 1997 alone there were 7713 cases where money allocated to particular programmes, for instance salaries to teachers, were used for other, often personal, purposes; 7 million roubles allocated for housing maintenance and more that 1 billion roubles allocated for the construction of accommodation for military officers have not been used accordingly.

Many of the oblast banks, which are delegated to handle Federal and oblast finances, also enjoy 'special relations' with the local administration. The lenient attitude of the oblast authorities allows them to slow down the flow of cash handled by them and thus earn sideways interest rates. There were over 40,000 cases of withheld payments to the staggering amount of 181 billion roubles (Ledin V., *Inter*, no. 27, 1997).

The oblast also owes 159 billion roubles in unpaid salaries and 243 billion roubles in unpaid child benefit (*ibid.*). The Federal government instructed the oblast to raise 50 per cent of this sum and promised to match it. However, the oblast is arguing over the respective shares, with the result that state employees such as teachers are not being paid for months at a time.

In order to circumvent the tough Federal monetary policy the oblast widely uses its own promissory notes. In 1994 there were 616 billion oblast promissory notes covering 1690 billion roubles of budget finances. This policy does not help in any way to establish hard budget constraints in the oblast economy.

Poor tax collection is also illustrated by the fact that 100,000 people, so-called 'chelnoky' (or shuttles) leave the oblast to go on business trips abroad, mostly to purchase goods in Turkey and the United Arab Emirates. None of them ever pays taxes on the profits, which often amount to thousands of dollars.

THE IMPACT ON FIRMS

The demise of communism and the changed relationships between centre and locality have had a substantial impact on individual firms. Control by the central industry ministry has gone and, with it, central funding. While individual enterprises were previously little more than production units and a minute component of the overall state plan, they are now largely independent and privatized. State funding for companies has virtually disappeared except for any remaining state orders, even though payment is not always forthcoming. Within firms the old system of 'management' (involving the Communist Party and the trades unions) has disappeared so that enterprises are now primarily driven by economic motivations.

At the same time horizontal political relationships with local administrations are being developed by companies in order to soften the transition. For their part local administrations are keen to exert their influence over economic developments. The municipal authority in Volgograd, for example, follows a protectionist policy, awarding contracts to local firms in an attempt to support local companies and make a contribution to the maintenance of employment and social stability.

Companies, moreover, have been exposed to the development of a market economy. This development is neither systematic nor even. While consumer markets have expanded, and have become openly competitive, industrial markets have evolved only slowly as companies have assisted each other and have been assisted by local administrations to stay alive. Capitalism has not necessarily resulted in open markets. Market institutions are still weak, including the monetary system which does not function (or functions only in part) for many companies which are obliged to use non-monetary instruments to effect and receive payment. The customs and practices of the past are also slow to die out in many areas as companies only gradually adjust to the new circumstances.

Many companies have also been adversely affected by the collapse of the former Soviet Union and COMECON. In the past inputs came from throughout the Soviet Union and COMECON; the same applied to customers. When the USSR broke down, many companies found that traditional suppliers and customers were now based in foreign countries. Trading with these companies now involved foreign currency transactions. The collapse of the USSR forced companies to rethink the links with their suppliers, as under communism these links no longer necessarily had the same economic rationale. In some cases the distances inputs had to be transported made them too expensive in the context of a market economy. In other cases companies could not obtain the foreign currency required for the purchase of raw materials. A similar situation applied to traditional customers: some were a long distance away in another part of Russia; others were now in foreign countries and did not want to, or could not afford to, buy the particular company's products.

In addition the price structure of inputs was changing. This might involve the item itself or its cost of transportation. All companies have been affected by the substantial rises in energy costs. The changing price of inputs is clearly helping to determine which products can be manufactured economically. Some companies, for example, have closed because of the realization that it was economically impossible for them to continue production.

In many instances the influence of the past has persisted into the present as the old political élites have regrouped, demonstrating considerable flexibility and adaptiveness. Local administrations also slow down the process of marketization by subsidizing local firms. Companies themselves attempt to re-establish former conditions of monopoly. Now that the Communist Party and KGB are no longer there to constrain and channel personal ambition (and greed), abuse is widespread (and is not necessarily illegal) (Sakwa, 1996:218–24). The change of system has created both opportunities and threats.

LOCAL ECONOMIC POLICY

Provinces and municipalities have, compared to the situation under communism, considerably enhanced powers. However, they have relatively few funds to implement economic policies. According to one member of the oblast Duma whom we interviewed, local economic policy consists of a few programmes which are largely based on old Communist Party thinking. These programmes contain little that is concrete (but much wishful thinking). Many people in the administration and in the Duma are prone to 'nostalgia'. Local economic policy is thus poorly developed. Furthermore many individuals who enter politics do so only to further their own interests and ambitions. In this respect the Volgograd Duma is no exception.

There is also considerable conflict between the oblast and the municipality. Respective powers and responsibilities are not clearly defined. The relationships between the Federation and the constituent members are also not yet clearly defined. To some degree the centre is adopting a policy of divide and rule, as conflict between oblast and municipality deflects attention from the Federal level. The tensions in the relationship between the oblast governor and the Federal representative in the oblast reflect the difficulty of the situation between Federation and province. While the oblast governor may refuse to ratify the implementation of Federal legislation in the oblast, the Federal representative has the right to declare a state of emergency.

All these aspects contribute to the complexity and diversity of economic life in the province. Elements of the market economy mingle with practices from the past. Increased power at provincial level does not necessarily lead to actions which support the development of a market environment. Capitalism has established itself but in many instances is based on abuse of political and market power. At the same time enterprises need to be restructured and reformed. How enterprises are responding to the new political and economic situation is the theme of the following chapters.

Part II
Case Studies

4 Industrial Dinosaurs

Part II of the book is concerned with an investigation of the different categories of company described in Chapter 1. This chapter focuses on the former giants of Soviet industry and begins with an account of the former state planning system which formed the basis for economic activity.

CENTRAL PLANNING

The history of central planning dates from 1928, when the first 5-year plan was introduced. Under the iron hand of Stalin the Russian economy had to 'leap forward' from a predominantly agrarian to an industrialized economy, capable of producing defence products which were technologically equal to those of the USA. As Stalin explained, in 10 years the USSR had to complete what market economies had taken hundreds to achieve.

With several variations Soviet central planning of the economy operated under a system of ministerial responsibility. Each individual enterprise belonging to a particular branch of industry was subordinated to a certain ministry. Before the demise of the USSR there were more than 60 ministries in which thousands of bureaucrats were fully responsible for enterprise performance, its suppliers and distributors. Parallel to ministries there were state committees which were in charge of the coordination of the work of the ministers. At the end of the 1980s there were 38 such committees.

The most influential of these state committees was Gosplan, or the State Planning Commission, which was responsible among other things for the administration, coordination and reconciliation of differences in enterprise requests and the formulation of the final plan, and then for issuing directives which were legally binding on all enterprises (Angressano, 1992:386). Additionally Gossnab, or the State Committee for Material and Technical Supply, was responsible for the allocation of enterprise inputs; Gosbank, or the state bank, was technically responsible for providing what later became known as soft budget constraints (Kornai, 1990). There was also the Central Statistical Administration (CSA) which was in charge of gathering economic data to monitor plan fulfilment. Parallel to this function the CSA was responsible (for prestige and ideological purposes) for concealing negative data about the state of the Soviet economy; for example by overstating the rate of economic growth and other indicators.

Goskomstsen, or the State Pricing Commission, was responsible for supervising and establishing prices for over 20 million different products. Once a price was established it remained rigid despite shifts in demand and supply. In fact often in the 1970s Soviet propagandists boasted that prices for major food products and rents were not only stable, but unchanged since the monetary reform of 1961. Another commission worth mentioning is Goskomtrud, or the State Commission for Labour and Social Questions, which determined the required number of professions, skills and the general quantity of labour required by the 5-year plan. Goskomtrud also determined the working conditions and monetary and non-monetary incentives required to encourage labour to relocate to climatically harsh areas of Siberia, and was also responsible generally for the social infrastructure of the Soviet Union.

According to the logic of the central planners, in this hierarchical system the enterprise occupied the lowest level (Gregory and Stuart, 1990:22). Above the enterprise was a monstrously huge bureaucracy of 10–15 million people. At the very top of this pyramid were just 15–20 people, who formed the Politburo of the Communist Party of the USSR and who made the political decisions on how the economy should be run, and who set its objectives. In fact, even the Politburo during Soviet history was often substituted by just one person, who happened to be at the top – either Stalin, Khrushchev or Brezhnev.

The simplicity of the central planning mechanism was illusionary. In reality it was an extremely complicated system overlapped with grey and shadow economies and heavy personal networking amongst its institutions and decision makers. If we ignore the cost of its achievements, we can admit that the central planning mechanism, as coordinator of all economic activity, has been rather effective, even though mistakes and drawbacks of the system were cushioned by the heroic and enthusiastic actions of the believers in the communist ideology. It was certainly effective in forcing development in selected high-priority areas.

However, over the more recent decades the Soviet economy became even more complex and revealed its limitations in delivering consumer goods, providing incentives and facilitating technological progress. The major problems of the planning mechanism according to Angressano (1992) were: firstly, bureaucratization of economic life which impinged upon individual incentive and failed to allow for consumer preferences – the result was overproduction of low-quality goods and a shortage of desired goods; secondly, the number of 'rukovoditelej' or hand-movers, in other words administrators, relative to workers was disproportionally high; thirdly, planning permitted the authorities to make decisions arbitrarily, compelling subordinates to follow directives which often lacked any economic rationale; fourthly, planning caused inflexibility in that adjustment to disequilibrium situations was slow; fifthly, enterprises and workers (who did not fear losing their jobs) were engaged in dysfunctional behaviour by responding to incentives that did not take profit maximization into account; finally, mistakes by planners were magnified throughout the economy.

In the conscience and behaviour of its economic agents 'the shunning of any individual incentive, the formal compliance with the political will expressed by the authorities, the cult of the overfulfilment of the plan, and the pervasive cheating and biasing of means and achievements' (Lavigne, 1995:22) were typical phenomena.

During the mid-1950s the Soviet Union's leadership made several attempts to make the economic system more efficient, without radically changing it. In the period 1965–7 Kosygin, prime minister in the Brezhnev government, introduced radical elements into the Soviet system taken from the arsenal of the market economy. Enterprise performance had to be evaluated by two major indicators: profitability and volume of sales. The hope was to combine plan and market together.

At that time it was not clear to Soviet economic policy makers that market criteria would not have any beneficial impact and would lose all economic meaning in the conditions of absolute state property ownership, state control over prices, central allocation of supplies and the dominant and unquestionable leading role of the Communist Party transmitted via numerous ministers. A quite justifiable fear of losing power and control prevented Soviet leaders from going too far in reforming the economy.

REFORMS AND THEIR CONSEQUENCES

By the mid-1980s it was obvious that any change in a failing economic system could not be accomplished without radical transformation of the political institutions. Gorbachev, in his naive attempts to make the Soviet socialist system work, started the most comprehensive of reforming processes.

The beginning of the changes which brought the Russian economy on to the path of the so-called transformation process from the centrally planned economy to the market can be dated as beginning in 1987, when two fundamental pieces of legislation were passed: one was the Law on State Enterprises, another the Law on Cooperatives. The first gave greatly expanded autonomy to enterprises, the second to individuals (Gaddy, 1996: 63). However, the traditional elements of the system, such as the soft budget constraint, state ownership of enterprise assets and state-controlled prices, remained intact. Enterprises received thousands of indicators and requests to fulfil hundreds of different monthly, quarterly and annual forms of bureaucratic inventiveness. In fact the new 5-year plan for 1986–90 was still being prepared on the basis of old assumptions and using the same traditional indicators.

Enterprises accustomed to limited independence were naturally keen to exploit (and abuse) the new opportunities granted them by the law, that is, of setting their own salaries and wages, and of converting the balances of their enterprises into cash. This situation, where on the one hand there continued to be tight state control over prices and on the other hand there was an opportunity for enterprises and individuals to increase cash incomes, could lead to only one thing – severe monetary overhang. The logical result of this situation was shortages in almost everything, but most striking of all, in foodstuffs. Queues became a common feature all over the Soviet Union and 'where there is no queue there is nothing on the shelves' (Dyker, 1992:172).

In 1991 the Soviet leaders officially admitted for the first time the existence of inflation in the system. In fact it was running at 140 per cent a year. The government moved to revitalize the economy by giving incentives to enterprises facing the problems 'such as the inconsistency between the *de jure* state ownership of most productive assets and *de facto* management control of most enterprise activities' (Ernst *et al.*, 1996:214).

The inertia of the old system, developed over more than 70 years of its existence, combined with the elements of the new, created substantial confusion about the best way forward. The real choice was somehow more limited: either to go back through repression to the old-type Soviet system, which still represented in the eyes of millions of Russians the lost security, non-conflict and paternalistic state attitudes, or to go fully to the creation of the market economy with its unemployment, inflation and long-forgotten reliance on one's own strengths and abilities.

After an initial push democratization and glasnost started their own logical development which, as it turned out, became uncontrollable, and which finished off not only the former communist politics and planned economy of the country, but the country itself. By the early 1990s the communists were speedily losing power. The failed 1991 coup completely discredited the Communist Party. The loss of its coercive powers brought about the dissolution of the Soviet Union. Russia was facing the situation where 'neither state bureaucracy nor market performed coordination functions in the economy' (Ernst *et al.*, 1996:214). By 1992, when the economic reform package was introduced by Gaidar's government, Russian industry was experiencing perhaps the most difficult period since the revolution of 1917.

Much has been written about shock therapy as tried by reformers and introduced by Gaidar in Russia. In this section we summarize the major points of the reform package and its results (Kotz and Weir, 1997). Minimum government involvement and maximum speed were the slogans of the reformers. The economic policy based on the shock therapy concept included the following elements: price liberalization, complete elimination of all elements and policies of resource allocation, privatization of state assets (enterprises and land), macroeconomic stabilization (balanced budget via reduction of government spending together with tight monetary policy), opening up of the economy to international trade and foreign direct investment.

Price liberalization, or in other words elimination of state control over prices, was supposed to make prices, set by the interaction of supply and demand, perform their main function as in the market economy, that is to signal to companies what to produce and how to produce with minimum cost.

Liberalized prices would be able to show what consumers really wanted. For goods in demand prices would go up, triggering a response among suppliers, that is, an increase in the production of that particular good. However, for goods which were not in demand prices would fall and producers would move their resources to the areas where prices for goods seemed to promise more fruitful returns.

The policy of macroeconomic stabilization was devised to slow down and then eliminate inflation. All public-sector programmes, subsidies to enterprises and military spending were severely curtailed. These measures were accompanied by sharp Central Bank actions to reduce money supply and growth of credit.

Rapid mass privatization had radically changed the economic foundations of society, turning state property into private property. It was obvious to the reformers that such a colossal task could not be accomplished overnight, especially in the case of large state enterprises. However, intermediate measures, such as conversion into joint-stock companies with the state as major shareholder, were foreseen. At a later date shares would be transferred to private shareholders.

The remaining mechanisms of the formerly mighty centrally planned economy were to be wiped out completely. The measures to achieve this included abolition of all governmental orders which required enterprises to produce a certain volume of output for the state, with the minor exception of the military–industrial complex. From now on market forces were the 'sole mechanism of coordination for the economy' (Kotz and Weir, 1997:163).

Free trade, and free inflow and outflow of capital, were the final items in the reformers' package. Import and export restrictions were to be eliminated both on foreign investment in Russia and on Russian investment abroad.

Shock therapy was intended to replace the old Soviet system as quickly as possible without using 'parts of the old system to help to construct the new one' (*ibid.*). The results of such revolutionary measures on Russian society and economy are extremely complicated and contradictory. Much has been written in the Russian and Western press analysing the results of this 6-year-old experiment. Opinions vary from extreme optimism to total rejection of what has been done to the Russian economy. Following this exposition of the former central planning system and its demise, we will now explore the impact of the reforms of the economic system though a case-study analysis of one of Volgograd's industrial companies – the Parts Plant.

THE PARTS PLANT: INDUSTRY BACKGROUND

The Parts Plant belongs to the agricultural machine-building industry. This means that for this company the situation in Russian agriculture is the major external influence with a direct effect on the company's well-being. The case study will thus begin with an analytical overview of the present state of Russian agriculture.

The inefficiency of Russian agriculture is striking, even in comparison to the rest of Russian industries. When compared with the European agricultural sector, Russian agriculture is five times more energy-intensive and requires four times the volume of metal-based resources. The state monopoly on international trade pumped enormous amounts of state credits into agriculture during the Soviet period. Additionally fixed, artificially low prices for agricultural machinery, in combination with managerial decisions based not on knowledge or common sense but on Communist Party directives, damaged the branch and further detracted from the efficiency of its constituent organizations.

Agricultural restructuring was seen as a significant break from old practices. As everywhere in industry the reformers applied free-market and monetarist economic theories to the problem of transforming a state socialist agricultural system into capitalist agriculture. Some of the first measures were the following: state subsidies were cut over a 5-year period from 66 billion roubles in 1991 to 8 billion in 1996. Agriculture received from the state budget in 1996 only 6 per cent of what it had received in 1991.

Like the 'Domino principle' the cuts have affected the related industries of tractor and agricultural machine-building. In 1996 16,000 tractors were purchased compared with 143,700 in 1990. During the same period, purchases of lorries fell from 97,600 to 5000. The purchase of grain combines fell from 37,800 to 5000. The decline in demand due to the lack of resources, liberalization of prices and the inability of companies to acquire market behaviour overnight, created a situation in which the agricultural machine-building industry shrank virtually day by day.

Between 1992 and 1997 industrial output declined much faster than in the rest of the Russian economy. In fact in 1996 industry was using only 14 per cent of its capacity. Compared with the pre-reform year of 1991 the production of tractors and grain combines fell almost nine-fold, of ploughs and seed-machines 23-fold and 28-fold respectively.

Approximately 30 per cent of employees in the industry had to go on involuntary holidays in 1996 and another 18 per cent, in the same year, worked a reduced working week. Considering the fact that the average salary in the agricultural machine-building industry is approximately 30 per cent lower than in the machine-building industry, many qualified workers left for good.

Absence of government financial support and an inability to raise its own finances brought about a situation in which there is no new investment in the industry. At the end of 1996 about half of all industrial plant was considered to be in need of urgent replacement. The extremely hard financial situation in agriculture was reflected in a drastic fall in the demand for agricultural machines; the decline does not allow machine-building enterprises to increase prices for their products as much as other industries can do.

For instance, the prices increased in agricultural machine-building for the period from 1991 to 1994 by 5237 per cent, but during the same period in non-ferrous industries prices increased by 19,684 per cent, in the petroleum industry by 13,139 per cent and in the electrical power industry by 12,649 per cent.

More than 30 per cent of the agricultural machine-building enterprises cannot cover the cost of production with their revenues. According to the Russian Ministry of Finance 93 per cent of industrial enterprises are in an unsatisfactory financial situation. Absence of working capital pushes companies into barter and mutual indebtedness, phenomena which are typical for most enterprises.

The complicated tax system also puts a burden on enterprises. After payment of all taxes the enterprise has only 9 kopecks left from each rouble of product sold. That is obviously not enough for innovations, investments and growth. But even if there were growth in industry, it would take at least 10 years to regain the 1991 level of production, a level which could hardly be called efficient (Agapsov, 1997:20).

COMPANY BACKGROUND

The history of the Parts Company dates from the end of the last century. In 1899 the French trading house Gardien et Vallos opened a subsidiary on the bank of the Volga River with the aim of producing bolts and bondings. By 1914 employment had almost tripled to 330 employees and production increased to 160,000 tons of bolts, nuts and chains. During the Russian Civil War, in 1918, the main power steam engine of the plant was blown up. However, soon after the war the plant was rebuilt, and from 1934 it become a subsidiary of the biggest tractor plant in Russia, which was named after Joseph Stalin. During the Second World War the plant produced armour for the Soviet Army; production included mines, shells and detonators. From 1947, on the decision of the Soviet Central Planning Committee, the Parts Plant again became independent from the Tractor Plant. In

1979, in recognition of its contribution to the fulfilment of the 5-year plan, it was honoured by being awarded the Red Banner of the Ministry of Tractor and Agricultural Machine Building. One-fifth of the company's equipment is less than 10 years old and approximately 50 per cent of the equipment is 20 years old or older. At the end of 1997 there were 2000 employees. The company produces 1800 different components: springs, nuts and bolts and some tool sets for tractor drivers. The enterprise's eight workshops spread over 19 hectares.

Prior to 1990 the Parts Company was supplying 130 manufacturing plants and 200 agricultural–technical units (baz sel'hoztechniky). The major users of the plant's products were tractor and engine factories in Russia, Belorussia, Ukraine, Kazakhstan and Uzbekistan. In 1995 just a fraction of the traditional users remained such as the Volgograd Tractor Factory, Minsk Tractor Factory, Pavlodar Tractor Factory (Kazakhstan) and Vladimir Tractor Factory.

There are no available market share statistics. However, the company knows it has major competitors: a company in Saratov and one in the Urals (Belibei) which are the main suppliers of similar products to the automotive industry as well as several subsidiaries of still-functioning metallurgical plants that have easier access to raw materials and consequently lower prices. There is also competition from Belorussia, Kazakhstan and the Ukraine.

In 1991 the decline started, and culminated in 1994, when the plant was producing just one-third compared to 1990 and selling only slightly more that half of its production. The reasons for the decline are very similar to what most of the country's industries were experiencing. The major causes which triggered the decline in output included: the collapse of the Soviet empire with accompanying losses of traditional suppliers and distributors, many of whom happened now to be in other republics, now independent countries; and the process of dismantling the institutions of the centrally planned economy without visible alternatives and lack of clarity over property rights (the enterprise was leased from the state). The situation, in which the directors felt themselves 'half owners' and thus, according to Gaidar, 'could steal from their dear enterprise calmly and shamelessly' (*Izvestia*, no. 186, 1997), but without having accompanying ownership responsibilities, was seriously damaging to the company.

In 1993 the new managing director decided to privatize the company. The new MD, in his early thirties and a former local Komsomol and later Communist Party leader, was full of ideas how to turn the company around. Having recently successfully defended his PhD thesis he was keen to put his ideas in practice. With him he brought his friend, who had substantial business experience, and the MD made him his deputy. In February 1993 the Parts Company became a joint-stock company.

OWNERSHIP AND CONTROL

The problems of privatization in Russia and the interrelationship between ownership and control have attracted much attention amongst researchers studying the Russian and East European transformation (e.g. Boyko, *et al.*, 1995; Frydman and Rapaczynski, 1994).

The dominant form of Russian privatization appears to be that of management and employee buy-outs, which contrasts with Western companies, in which such forms are the exception rather than the rule. Our research in this field also shows a strong union of the new ownership and old control as opposed to the conventional Western practice of the separation of ownership and control.

Under the 1991 Law on Privatization, industrial enterprises could be privatized in such a way that, initially, the major shareholder would be the State Property Committee, under which 25 per cent of the claims on the company assets would be given free of charge to the employees and 5 per cent could be purchased by the management. However, the communists in the federal Duma, the Russian parliament, in Autumn 1992 proposed and pushed through a different option for privatization. According to this route the labour collectives of the enterprise were allowed to purchase up to 51 per cent of the enterprise assets while an additional 5 per cent would be available for purchase with the enterprise funds. The remaining shares were held by the State Property Committee which had eventually to sell them at cash and voucher auctions.

Obviously this latter option gave far more control together with ownership to managers. But as Gaidar once said, 'We were willing to conduct privatization playing even by the communists' rules as long as privatization was going ahead ... the choice between quality of privatization and speed was made in favour of the latter' (*Izvestia*, no. 186, October 1997).

The management of the Parts Company persuaded workers to choose the second route under which the danger of the sale of the shares to outsiders was minimized. In fact, according to Bim (1996), 83.3 per cent of newly created joint-stock companies (transformed state enterprises) had followed this path. The percentage for all industrial enterprises is estimated as only slightly lower.

At the time of conducting this research there were six major shareholders with one internal individual investor owning 20 per cent of the company's shares. The management was reluctant to name them, and only through indirect sources of information could the authors ascertain that the major shareholder is allegedly the director himself, with only 12 per cent of the shares belonging to the employees.

During 1993–6 the management of the Parts Company acquired further shares from workers, who sometimes did not appreciate the significance of possessing them. There have been no dividend payments so far, and this has contributed to the workers' indifference to keeping them. Approximately 20 per cent of the shares belong to outsiders, and again it was quite difficult to find out their identity. However, some sources indicated that external shareholders include two major local banks (one is currently under federal criminal investigation) and individual shareholders belonging to the local elite and the local authorities. About 5 per cent of the non-voting shares were purchased via vouchers by former, now-retired workers of the enterprise. An almost-identical situation was discovered at three other industrial enterprises. We believe that this reinforces Simon Clarke's observation that 'far from subjecting enterprises to the control of outside owners, share auctions have served to cement relationships between industrial enterprises, financial structures and political bodies' (Clarke, 1996:42).

In spite of the fact that, according to the Law on Privatization, closed joint-stock companies, like those outlined above, were declared illegal, in effect many enterprises, especially those which have chosen the second route to privatization (and these enterprises are in the majority), retained insider control over the enterprise. In this context, Bim (1996:473) observes that: 'The main distinction between Russian insider ownership and the classical model of collective ownership is the absolutely predominant role of managers in governance and control over Russian privatized enterprises that are formally owned by all categories of insiders'.

Often the management of the enterprise does everything possible to prevent outsider ownership, even if it could bring immediate benefits to the company. There was a typical example of this kind of behaviour recently in the Kirov Textile Factory. When Americans expressed an interest in investing in the company, but conditioned the investment by intending to acquire the controlling package of the

claims on the company's assets, the director of the enterprise successfully appealed to the patriotic feeling of the workers, using phrases
such as 'Americans are buying out our Motherland' and 'You will all
be on the streets and American robots will do the job.' The labour
collectives, in spite of the attractive offer which could have changed
the enterprise's future, rejected American involvement (*Argumenty i
Fakty*, no. 48, 1998).

According to the Head of Human Resources Management at the
Tractor Parts Company, the 'privatization and the sale of the shares
did not raise capital but commitment' and that is 'the stimulus for the
management and the workers to work effectively and responsibly'.
However, ordinary employee shareholders are much more sceptical.
So far, they have not received any dividends and, as under the old
regime, they do not have a say in the enterprise's affairs. So when the
management of the company offers to buy the employees' shares for
cash, the offer is rarely rejected. The managers explained the policy
of obtaining the controlling stake of the shares in terms of the fear of
losing control to outsiders. Interestingly, employees expressed the
same concern, but the concentration of the shares in the hands of
their own managers was not perceived by them as threatening.

FINANCIAL CONSTRAINTS

The radical reform measures designed to put an end to the soft
budget constraints and price liberalization, combined with uncontrollable money supply during the first 2 years of the reform, created
major payment difficulties for Russian enterprises. In effect these
measures wiped out their existing working capital. Remarkably,
however, the reaction of Russian industrial enterprises to the government policy of economic austerity, aimed at introducing financial
discipline, differed from what was expected.

The firms' reactions to a total lack of working capital brought about
a situation of mutual indebtedness through debtor networking which
allowed technically bankrupt firms to survive. According to Clarke
(1996:35) the debts of Russian companies amounted to around 78
trillion roubles at the end of 1994; debts to suppliers accounted for
52 trillion roubles, with the remainder owed to the tax authorities,
banks and employees.

The situation at the Parts Company confirms this general picture.
It owes its suppliers (including energy costs) 19,767 million roubles,

whilst 4452 million is owed to them by their major customers. There are overdue bank loans for 1.1 million roubles and overdue budget payments for 5207 million roubles. The is also a 2–3-month deferral in the payment of wages, which is blamed on the shortage of cash. Some workers have told us that they believe that the management is holding down their wages intentionally to 'patch the holes in the firm's budget'. However, according to them, they cannot prove it because they do not have access to company documentation. As one worker put it: 'We do not understand their [managers'] finances and even if we did, there are hundreds of ways they can fool us.'

At the same time workers were praising their managers, saying that their bosses are better than others. Often, instead of monetary wages, they are given bricks from the local construction firm with which the company exchanges bolts and nuts to maintain earth-moving machinery. There is much private construction going on in the city. Thus, bricks are quite easily turned into cash. The share of barter in sales at the company has risen since 1992 and now represents approximately 40 per cent of total sales.

To ease the cash problem, the company has opened its own store where it can sell its barter items to consumers, directly. The variety of goods in the store is quite staggering: from bicycles to PVC and kitchen knives. There is also a department at the store which sells alcohol. The managing director proudly told us that it was his idea: 'You know, Russians tend to celebrate when they buy something and instead of going somewhere else, we can offer them what they are looking for to make the purchase complete.'

In fact the shop is a cash generator. There is already work going on to open another two shops on the company's premises. The expected profit from this kind of activity, when all shops are opened, is estimated at US$200,000. The realities of this and other companies which have been studied, show that Russian managers can really be very innovative.

PROFIT MOTIVE

Profit in the Western sense suggests the presence of capital, a financial infrastructure and a quantitative evaluation system, all of which barely exist within the Russian context. There is no conventional profit motive because there is no money in the enterprises. The degree of company indebtedness is so great that it distorts any meaningful financial appraisal of the company's position. The current tax regime militates against the earning of profits. During our research, all interviewed managers gave the impression that they identified with the future of their enterprises. However, based on some implicit information and the findings of other researchers (e.g. Bim, 1996) we would suggest that the extraction of personal wealth from the enterprises is one of the strongest motives for them to be in business. This can be viewed as normal behaviour. However, this wealth extraction is done in a way which is harmful to the enterprise. The income generated by the leasing of enterprise equipment and the premises often goes directly into senior managers' pockets and not into investment in the company itself.

ENTREPRENEURISM AND LEGALITY

Another common way of extracting rent for top managers is the opening up of peripheral businesses which use the equipment and the premises of technically bankrupt companies. All of the enterprises where the research was conducted had at least one small business on their territory. In one case there were three. The plot is quite simple. The technically bankrupt enterprise cannot pay for energy. It also cannot pay any property tax. However, the peripheral business, using the 'free' equipment and 'free' energy inputs, produces goods which can be sold for cash. The profit is usually shared between managers. Often, to avoid problems of profit distribution and conflict, the directors of a peripheral business are frequently relatives of the managing directors. On one occasion, during a luxurious dinner with plenty of expensive fish, caviar and vodka, the top manager of an enterprise, which had not paid its workers for 5 months, hinted that the 'associated' business run by his relative could allow him to give dinners of this kind every day.

One of the major frauds of this kind has currently attracted particular attention in the Russian mass media. It is the case of the technically bankrupt Russian railways and its profitable subsidiary Transrail, run by the son of the railway's managing director. Transrail makes an annual profit of US$350 million and the total value of profit extracted from the company is estimated at US$4 billion (*Izvestia*, no. 19, 1997:2). In this connection we quite agree with Alexander Bim's observation that 'in the Russian transition situation the wealth of managers is all too often built up not on efficient company performance or restructuring but on deliberate and semi-legal capital extraction' (Bim, 1996).

MANAGEMENT STRATEGY TOWARDS SOCIAL ASSETS OF THE ENTERPRISE

The role which the enterprise's social assets played in the former communist system was extremely important. Non-monetary benefits, of which the Soviet enterprise was a major provider, were an important source of employee motivation especially when the rouble, due to shortages of goods, could not be converted even internally. Non-monetary benefits also were designed to 'attract and retain scarce skilled labour providing [*sic*] a powerful lever of managerial influence over the labour force' (Clarke, 1996:28).

The Parts Company was no exception. The enterprise provided its own kindergarten (it has had to transfer two others to the local authority because of cuts in the labour force). There were also two dormitories for single mothers and married couples, a recreational camp on the Volga River and a health check clinic. In spite of the current difficulties, the management has not even questioned the necessity of having these social assets. As one of the managers put it: 'of course we could probably sell them, but the workers will not understand us. When the state has completely withdrawn from having any concern about its people, our social assets are even more important for our workers than was the case in the past.'

The collapse of state residential construction programmes made the dormitories belonging to enterprises extremely valuable assets. Approximately 300 workers live there at the moment, and the prospects of them getting their own accommodation are very grim. To rent privately is extremely costly. On average it could take two-thirds of an average monthly salary for a one-bedroom apartment. So for those who use the company's dormitories, to lose a job would mean that they would have to move out.

The company's recreational facilities are used currently only for entertaining 'useful people'. These could be MPs from the city parliament (Duma), a big customer or the top management themselves and their families. As for workers, they probably use them only for a weekend during summer time. Approximately one-third of the labour force has spent at least 4 months on 'involuntary vacation' due to the fall in demand, so that most employees as a rule try to earn some money during their legal holidays. According to the human resources manager, more than 80 per cent of workers and 60 per cent of managers have not had a vacation for the past 3 years.

EXTERNAL TRADE RELATIONS

Widespread mutual indebtedness, lack of cash and inability to pay for needed products moved many companies into looking for foreign buyers who would pay cash. Because of the relative cheapness of Russian labour companies believed that selling abroad would not represent a big challenge. Quality was believed to be the major factor which needed to be improved. The reality was somehow more complicated. Putting the quality issues aside, two major obstacles are facing the company.

Firstly, in spite of the much lower cost of labour, the Western prices for similar products are actually lower than Russian prices. Compared to prices for similar products offered by Singapore, India or China the difference can be up to four times! The reason lies in very high prices for production inputs such as electricity and steel, the price of which is high due to high electricity prices. Transport costs are also twice as high as internationally.

Secondly, the company has problems in meeting Western standards on packaging, which has hitherto not been an issue for Russian companies. It had just never been considered important. The chief engineer of the company gave the authors a recent example illustrating the problem. The company recently found a buyer in Iran and sent 65 tons of nuts and bolts. In order to meet the Iranian requirement on packaging the company had urgently to find a local packaging company which made 2000 boxes out of natural timber at prices equivalent to 2 tons of the products.

According to the Head of Quality Control, 'quality is also an issue, but at least this problem depends on us. It is hard to achieve it without sophisticated monitoring equipment, but still we can, if we really want to. For the Iran contract we had to produce twice as many nuts and bolts in order to achieve the required output to meet the Iranian side's DIN standard but we did it. But we cannot influence the crazy prices we pay for electricity.'

In fact in the cost structure of production the cost of electricity is about 30 per cent, compared to 13–15 per cent for labour. The Head of Quality Control was moreover right in saying that the price of electricity cannot be changed. What can be changed, however, and what has changed, is the attitude to its use. In order to lower the cost of electricity inputs in production, most of production takes place after 11 a.m., to avoid the peak-time tariff, and during the night. The decision to change the traditional working hours has been approved by the majority of employees.

INSTITUTIONAL RELATIONS

Under the old system the Soviet enterprises constituted an integral part of the local district. Social facilities belonging to the enterprise, such as kindergartens, dormitories and enterprise housing provided to its own workers, were concentrated in the close vicinity of the enterprise. Lack of an effective transport infrastructure and individual transport also influenced the situation in which, as a rule, workers lived around their enterprises. In Volgograd even the districts in which big enterprises were situated were named after them, i.e. Traktorozavodskij, Barrikady, Metiznij, etc. Through informal and formal networking, usually reinforced by the local Communist Party committee, the enterprises had to take an active part in the organization of public services and amenities. Streets had to be cleaned regularly, roads and houses maintained, banners put up during the official celebrations. The collapse of the one-party system, together with its mechanism of forcing enterprises to take care of the district where they were situated, and combined with the mass of problems at the enterprises themselves, put an end on the whole to the role of the enterprise in social and leisure activities.

Between 1992 and 1997 the district infrastructure deteriorated greatly. However, the people's expectation of the positive role which the enterprise should play in the district's well-being is still very high. Local politicians understand the importance for people of the local public services and amenities, and try to use their influence on enterprises, forcing them to find the resources needed to continue this role. Interestingly, there is now no formal mechanism which could be used by the city authorities to put pressure on enterprises. However, very often newly elected MPs and new managing directors are of similar age, experience and educational background. They have got their positions on the waves of the changes which swept across Russia during the reform years. In the case of the Parts Plant the managing director knew personally at least half of the local MPs, some of whom graduated from the same university as he did.

Local authorities also have other means of exercising their influence over enterprises. The most powerful means include the distribution of salaries and investment coming from the state budget. Also, local authorities are in close contact with the local tax offices which are feared by even the 'cleanest' of enterprises. The tax inspectors enjoy substantial power. For instance, they can freeze the bank accounts of suspected enterprises even without a court order. At the same time they themselves are subject to control by the local authorities. The management policy of the Parts Company towards the local district authorities takes account of these issues. As the managing director expressed it: 'We would like people to know that we are concerned about the city and our district. It is good for our public relations. We do what we can. We do not have funds but we often help the district with our labour and transport.'

At the same time, to have good working relations with local authorities is important but no longer critical. If in the past directors of even huge enterprises were vulnerable before the local regional Communist Party committee or communist city authorities, now they feel the power of being the owners. Their status and jobs can no longer be taken away by some communist bureaucrat. However, for some bureaucrats this loss of power is unbearable. One of the directors of the largest industrial enterprise in Volzhsky, a satellite city near Volgograd, recalls that when the major of Volzhsky came to him asking for several million roubles to close some holes in the city budget, he refused to do it. In response he heard bitterly: 'You would have been stripped of your communist party membership if you had answered like that in the past' (*Press Klub*, no. 11, 1997:3).

LABOUR RESTRUCTURING

According to conventional neoclassical wisdom the drastic fall in production has to be followed by a corresponding fall in employment. The reaction of Russian enterprises, especially at the initial stage of the reform, was to produce for the warehouse, without laying off workers. National statistics show that in 1992 enterprise inventories amounted to 16 per cent of Russian GDP. The experience of the Parts Company confirms the national trend. Approximately 20–30 per cent of what was produced was stored in 1994. This situation is explained by Clarke (1996:44), who observes that 'the absence of mass unemployment is one of the most striking features of the Russian transition'.

However, the process of redundancy has started. Employment at the company went down from 3500 employees in 1992 to 2000 in 1997. However, the cuts do not seem proportionate to the fall in production, considering that in 1992 the company was processing 100,000 tons of metal and in 1997 it processed only 30,000. According to the human resources manager, 'It was very difficult to get used to the idea of saying goodbye to people. It took us two to three years to understand that the enterprise just cannot survive without cuts. Some people were hysterical. We did not have any experience at all of how to handle the redundancies.'

Interestingly, the Head of Human Resource Management is the former plant Communist Party secretary. He still believes that the communists meant well, it is just 'the people who were not up to communism's ideas'. His rich past experience of working with people turned out to be a valuable asset in his new job. He knows almost everybody at the enterprise by their first name; with many older workers he had had contacts outside of the workplace. In fact throughout Russia, being a former communist does not have in itself the negative connotations so often visible in the Baltic states or the Czech Republic or even in Moscow. This is also partly due to the fact that many members of the Volgograd oblast Duma are communists and the oblast has a communist mayor.

As one way out of the human resource dilemmas, the enterprise decided to give redundant workers plots of land for dachas. The company had bought 1000 plots and now handed them to redundant workers who could use them to help feed themselves. The management of the company believes that the redundancy process is almost over. During the past 6 months there had been only one redundancy. The criteria for redundancy were eventually laid down in state regulations which help human resources managers greatly. The management believes that the employment strategy is clear for the next couple of years. The company does not expect an increase in demand and wants to raise the existing level of skill and training of the employees. Many interviewees mentioned a phrase which reflects their attitude to the problem of recruitment: 'the wisdom of the old and the enthusiasm of the young'.

MOTIVATION

According to interviewed managers the major motivating factor is the fear of losing one's job. If in the past people were concerned primarily with their salaries, and then with social benefits offered by the enterprises such as the possibility of getting a flat, or the opportunity of having good recreational facilities or child care, now motivation is more straightforward. The company now has its own recruitment procedure and places new employees on probation for 3 months. Many interviewees indicated that their motivation lies in a belief in the company's future, which people associated with the MD and his team.

However, according to one of the managers: 'Fear is not good enough.' The company tries to revive some of the old traditions belonging to the communist past. One of them is celebration of the 'Day of the Machine-builders'. In fact in the Soviet Union all professions had a day named after their profession. It was not a holiday, but still at the appropriate enterprises people would celebrate, with some taking a half-day off. The authors happened to be at the enterprise on the Day of the Machine-builders. There was a free concert organized by the employees together with some members of their families, and a free company lunch. The administrative headquarters were decorated, using probably the decoration they had, symbols left over from the communist past such as red banners and red artificial poppies.

The company has its own award. It seems that the old tradition of giving good employees so-called 'moral awards' is also on the increase at the enterprise. In the past it was common to have picture stands with photographs of the best workers. During the perestroika years this practice was ridiculed as inefficient and outdated, and it has not been used for some years. However, now the attempt to revive it appeared to be very successful. So a new picture stand has been built and new photographs were displayed on it. Probably the major and obvious difference was that instead of officially grim faces (as in the past) the new photographs are of much more relaxed and smiling people. Employees seem to be happy to have this discontinued practice back.

TRAINING AND DEVELOPMENT

The company also has its own qualifications and has currently been focusing on management. All managers were asked to draw up their own development plans, which were approved by the head of the human resources department and will be used next year during the

annual personnel appraisal procedure. The major company requirements for training and development lie in the areas of industrial
marketing and distribution. There is no one at the enterprise with a
professional education in these areas. Unfortunately Russian experience in these areas is very weak. So the major marketing courses
offered by Volgograd's academic institutions are based on the works
of the famous American marketeer Philip Kotler. However, as
mentioned by one of the interviewees, 'Russia's current realities seem
to be focused on problems unknown to the western text-books.'

QUALITY CONTROL TRAINING

Following advice from the Moscow Academy of Management, a
quality control division was set up in the company, comprising the
department of technical control, methodology department, central
plant laboratory, and documentation centre dealing with internal
auditing and process standards.

Some of the results of the new quality control system have been
reflected in the absence in 1997 of legal complaints from buyers,
compared to 20 such complaints in the previous year. Customers'
suggestions, or other more subtle expressions of buyer dissatisfaction,
have also declined by 50 per cent. The major changes, however,
according to the Head of Quality Control, are not in the formal structures but in the workers' attitudes: 'They [employees] understand now
that their well-being depends on sales and sales now depend not on
Moscow or the quantity of expensive fish brought by the company
director to Moscow's planning bureaucrats, but on the quality of
products manufactured by them.'

The Head of Quality Control is trying to implement voluntary
participation in quality circles: this, according to him, greatly
increased the involvement and satisfaction felt by individuals and also
their status. The quality process is perceived as bottom-up. Shop-
floor workers are apprised of the philosophy of quality control, while
supervisors concern themselves with the technical details.

Training people in quality control is the major theme in the
company's training programmes. Led by the Head of Quality Control
the programme is being implemented with the cooperation of the
local branch of the Russian Academy of Quality Control. The vice-
president of the Academy is a foreign expert and consultancy is free.
There is also a regional programme for quality control which is

chaired by the head of the regional administration together with the local Chamber of Commerce. Recently in Volgograd there was a fair, including the leading Western quality control institutions such as Lloyds and TÜV. Priority number one for the company is to achieve ISO 9000 by the end of the summer of 1998. The standard, according to the company managers, will greatly help to open Western markets for the enterprise's products.

STRATEGY TOWARDS THE TRADE UNIONS

The Soviet-type of trade union (TU), obediently modelled by the rest of the Eastern European countries with the exception of Poland, was integrated into the party and the management apparatus, fulfilling the role of one of the hands of the Communist Party enterprise committee (partkom). In the past the TU, on the one hand, was responsible for the allocation of the numerous social and welfare benefits to the employees and, on the other, had to motivate workers to work harder via socialist competition (socialisticheskoe sorevnovanie). By using its powers in the allocation of flats, places in usually overcrowded kindergartens, distribution of the virtually free recreational vouchers, the TU could influence working morale and encourage the growth of productivity. However, their seemingly powerful role was illusionary, as it could not function without the consent of the enterprise Communist Party committee.

The role of the TU at the Parts Company is changing. The interviews indicated that there is an element of scepticism towards it. The majority of employees believe that the union's role has decreased because there is no 'socialist competition' to encourage any more. Additionally, there are not many social goods to allocate. The greatest disillusionment concerning the union's role comes from the realization that unions cannot influence wages and salaries. Workers' discipline, which had been one of the major concerns of the TU, is no longer seriously affected by the discriminatory administration of the social and welfare functions of the plant. The fear of losing one's job is now a strong enough factor.

However, the trade union leader takes an active part in the redundancy procedures, often advising the HRM managers on legal matters. But this role is more that of a supporter of the company administration. During the past 5 years nobody could recall any incident when the TU had confronted the senior management of the enterprise. As one of the workers who had been with the enterprise for almost 20 years told us, expressing probably the extreme view of some of his colleagues: 'We do not care a damn about them [the TU]. They were parasites before, getting the best of the social goods for themselves and their relatives and now they play along with managers. If all of them disappear, we would not notice.'

Nevertheless, in spite of this attitude, the majority of employees are still trade union members. As one worker put it: 'It does not cost us to be members, but still there is a hope that they can help somehow. My children are small and there is a New Year tree and some small presents for them. Getting out of the union does not change anything, why bother then.'

In 1993 the TU did take an active part in the debates on the form of privatization. One of the reasons could be that the then trade union leader (Predsedatel Profkoma), who had been working in this role for 15 years, is currently one of the company's shareholders.

COMPANY STRATEGY FOR THE FUTURE

There are obvious attempts to turn the enterprise round and make it financially and technologically sound. The Parts Company has developed a strategy to escape from the existing crisis. This strategic programme includes:

- increasing the volume of working capital by negotiating post-ponements in the payment of loans, seeking new loans, raising volume of cash earned (both in the form of prepayments and sales) and improving debt collection;

- formulating a strategy based on marketing strategy and linked to distribution;

- increasing sales by identifying new customers, reviving old ties and developing a distribution network for the region and the 'near abroad';

- improving cost-effectiveness of operations;

- linking labour costs to product volume and quality and raising labour productivity through training and appraisal;

- implementing a social policy to support employees and their children – this requires increased funding for the kindergarten, children's pioneer camp and for company sport and library facilities and subsidies for catering.

The strategic programme contains a range of broad statements (with hardly any mention of how the programme is to be implemented). It also confirms the observation made by Tatiana Dolgopiatova (quoted in Rutland, 1996) that Russian firms are hybrid institutions, with one foot in the old planned economy and the other in the emerging market environment.

5 The Military Enterprises: Conversion or Destruction

INTRODUCTION

The construction of the Soviet state and its later disintegration are inseparable from the creation of the monstrous machine of its totalitarian regime known as the military industrial complex (MIC). We are in agreement with the opinion that 'the Soviet Union did not have a military industrial complex (MIC), it was one' (Mikheyev, 1996:134).

In fact one of the indisputable achievements of the centrally planned economy was its MIC. Day and night, in peacetime and during wars, the Soviet military machine worked without rest. All the country's natural resources, all its rich intellectual potential were placed at the service of the MIC. According to some Russian sources 60 per cent of the scientific potential of the country was directly or indirectly related to the arms sector.

The MIC was given a leading role in the plans of all Soviet leaders, with the sole exception, possibly, of Gorbachev. The monstrous baby of the MIC was conceived by Lenin and subsequently was bought up by Stalin, who believed in world revolution and the inevitability of military conflict between the 'progressive' communist world and decaying capitalism.

The huge propaganda machine of the Soviet Union tried to convince the rest of the world that the Soviet Union was the most peace-loving of countries, surrounded by trigger-happy capitalists. Enormous losses during the Second World War and the suffering of the Russian people were put forward as arguments for the Soviet Union not wanting war. The cost of the Second World War was really staggering, but this does not negate the fact that Stalin, as pointed out by many Russian historians (Radsinsky, 1997; Suvorov, 1996) all his life had a 'great dream': world revolution brought about by Soviet bayonets.

To fulfil this 'great dream' the dissemination of ideological dogmas was not enough. The Soviet Union had to have a military machine

81

capable of dragging mankind into the glorious communist future; and everything, all the country's major economic and political decisions, were influenced by this view.

After Stalin's death, and especially during Brezhnev's period of economic stagnation, the doctrine of 'one Soviet nation/one Soviet country in the whole world' began to look more and more absurd. In the 1960s and 1970s Marxism–Leninism was 'enriched and further developed' by Khrushchev's and later Brezhnev's doctrine of 'peaceful coexistence'. The idea of creating 'The United Soviet States', as Trotsky had originally called it, had been totally abandoned.

However, the inertia of the military machine, reinforced by the overwhelming power of the military lobby in the USSR, was so great that, in spite of the faltering economy, the country continued to produce mountains of deadly armour. The status of the Soviet Union, especially in its last years, 'was based almost entirely on its formidable military machine' (Levada, 1992:47).

A machine it was! In spite of the fact that the true size of the MIC will most likely never be discovered, some indicators allow us to appreciate its gigantic proportions. In the mid-1980s Gorbachev stated (understated?) that military expenditure accounted for 18 per cent of the national income (Ellman, 1993:23). Of course this figure represents only the direct costs, and excludes the cost of (using the official Soviet language) the so-called 'peaceful development of space' or in other words numerous and expensive space military programmes. Nor does it include the opportunity cost or the cost of the military 'friendly aid' provided to allied pro-communist movements and regimes.

The foundations of the MIC comprised nine branches of the Soviet defence industries, i.e. aviation, communications, defence, electronics, general machine-building, machine-building, medium machine-building, and radio and shipbuilding, involving between 2000 and 4000 production enterprises, research and development facilities and research institutes. Estimates of the number of people who worked in these organizations during their heyday range from 9 million to 14 million (O'Prey, 1995:15).

In 1989 the Soviet defence sector manufactured 1700 tanks (2.3 times as many as the United States), 300 multiple rocket launchers (6.2 times as many as the United States), 750 units of self-propelled artillery (19 times as many as the United States), 5700 armoured fighting vehicles (8.8 times as many as the United States) and 140 inter-continental ballistic missiles (11.1 times as many as the United

States). Between 1965 and 1990 the defence sector in the Soviet Union produced 100,000 tanks (more than the rest of the world combined) and 243 nuclear-powered submarines (22 times more than were produced by the rest of the world) (Mikheyev, 1996:134).

After the collapse of the Soviet Union Russia inherited from 60 to 80 per cent of the former state's MIC (O'Prey, 1995; Mikheyev, 1996). Considering the veil of secrecy over any statistics about the MIC the estimates vary even among top Russian officials. According to Ivan Silaev, the former prime minister of Russia (in office in 1992), 75 per cent of Russian industry was related to the military; according to Anatoli Chubais, 63 per cent. Other analysts estimate that the MIC consumed up to 80 per cent of Russia's raw materials and technical, financial and intellectual resources. In the middle of 1993 the Russian MIC was employing 6 million people and had 1400 factories and 967 research institutes.

In order to hide the major activities of the MIC, such as production of military goods, and disguise the statistics, the MIC also produced some civilian products such as radios, civilian aircraft, TVs, VCRs, refrigerators, tape recorders and sewing machines. In fact the amount of civilian goods produced by military enterprises was quite substantial. The majority of the country's industrial equipment and equipment for the agricultural sector and food-processing industries were produced at military enterprises. Interestingly, products for civilian consumption used to be dispatched during the day and the military goods during the night.

Military production dominated the entire Soviet civil economy. In fact the civil economy 'was negatively affected by the requirement that it actively serve the militarization of the economy' (Gaddy, 1996:40). According to Gaddy civil industrial production had to conform to military specifications. So tractors, aeroplanes and other civilian products were manufactured with possible military use in mind, often meeting the requirements not of the civil sector but of the defence sector.

All civilian technologies were also designed in a such a way that they could be converted into the manufacture of military products with minimum delay. As a result, because of their universality these 'universal machines' were less effective than if they had specialized only in the production of specific civilian goods. Maximum compatibility of the components which could be used both in military and civil products was another rule which negatively affected civil industries. The military would select the best parts or products which met the required military specifications. As for the rest, which was not up to the rigorous standards of the military, those parts would find their way into civil products. In general the parts or goods rejected by the military were of much better quality than average civilian ones; that is, unless these goods were produced for export, which required much superior quality compared with production for the domestic market.

Another indication of the vital importance of the MIC was reflected in its extremely privileged position within the economic structure of the former USSR. In an economy plagued by shortages the MIC never had problems with either capital or human inputs. The MIC had access to all the very best which was available in the Soviet economy. If in Stalin's times top managers and scientific and skilled workers were commanded where to work, subsequently the quality labour force and managers were attracted to the MIC by tangible and intangible benefits which were unheard of in the civil sectors of the economy. The defence enterprises had access to special recreational facilities, accelerated allocation of housing, cars and good-quality Russian or foreign consumer goods. The best graduates were selected by military representatives and according to the conventional practice at that time (robota po raspredileniu) were sent to work for at least 3 years in the places where they were considered to be most useful.

However, enormous military spending, priority over the civil sector and attempts to achieve military superiority at all costs 'were such a burden on the economy that they undermined the society the military expenditure was supposed to protect' (Ellman, 1993:23).

THE REGIONAL DIMENSION

After the collapse of the USSR Russia inherited the major share of the MIC. In terms of employment in the defence sector 71.2 per cent of total USSR defence complex employment was in Russia, although Russia accounted for only slightly more than half of the total population of the USSR (Gaddy, 1996:18–19). About 900 out of the 1100 military–industrial enterprises and 800 out of 920 R&D institutes of the former USSR are located in Russia.

The defence industries were typical features of most Russian cities. In the majority of large and small cities and towns in the Russian province there were closed zones or so-called 'jaschics' (boxes) where hundreds of thousands of people worked without being allowed to disclose what kind of goods they were producing. The idea of concentration and specialization, deformed by the centrally planned economy, took material form in the creation of enterprises of immense size. Within the defence industries there were approximately 100 enterprises with more than 10,000 employees (O'Prey, 1995:20).

Because of the secrecy of defence work there were whole cities built around military enterprises. Millions of workers and their families lived and worked behind tightly secured gates. They could not leave the gates of their cities, they could not have a holiday where they wanted and were allowed to visit only the special, albeit often very good, closed resort areas around the Black Sea to which they would be allocated. Interestingly enough, very many Russians considered themselves fortunate when they obtained a job in the MIC.

The closed cities often did not have proper names, but just coded numbers which sometimes resembled the names of existing Russian cities such as Cheliabinsk-20, Perm-10, etc. Even during general censuses of the population Russian statistics did not include the populations of these cities, which resulted in paradoxical demographic statistics.

The concentration of the Russian defence industries was rather uneven, with a substantial difference between oblasts. Some of the Russian oblasts relied very heavily on military contracts from the government. Six Russian oblasts were dependent upon the defence industries for more that 40 per cent of their industrial employment. The majority of Russia's defence industries is concentrated in a belt stretching from the western border eastward to western Siberia.

THE DEFENCE INDUSTRIES OF VOLGOGRAD OBLAST

The economy of Volgograd oblast was not a part of the so-called hypermilitarized economy. In fact the whole of the Povolzhsky region, with the exception of Samara oblast with one-quarter of its labour working in the defence industries, is rather 'military average'. However, in the Russian context, to be just average still meant that up to 10 per cent of the population was involved in military production or military R&D.

At least one-quarter of all Volgograd oblast's enterprises were directly or indirectly involved in the MIC. The proportion increases to up to half in Volgograd city. All major enterprises in the city had special manufacturing lines, the output of which was removed and tested by people in uniform. Numerous enterprises, in spite of their peaceful names, produced deadly weapons for the Soviet military machine. For example, the famous Volgograd Tractor Plant produced not only tractors for agriculture, which were made in such a way that they could be converted for military purposes, but pure military machinery including vehicles well known in military circles, such as tanks and other assault vehicles. Moreover, according to the authors' estimations, there were at least 10 major enterprises in Volgograd in which military production represented a majority of the total output. An enterprise with the neutral-sounding name 'Chimprom' (or chemical industry) would also produce poisonous gases, a shipbuilding company, as well as civilian ships, would also produce submarines.

THE IMPACT OF THE ECONOMIC REFORMS ON THE MIC

The economic reforms and the dramatic change in Russian foreign policy hit the MIC most severely. Until recently it was considered 'immoral and unpatriotic to question the absolute priority of the defence of the motherland, and every idea of calculating the cost of such defence was implicitly suspect' (Gaddy, 1996:3).

The democratic changes in Russia brought about a realization among the reformers of the fact that the quantity of the MIC's production was not really necessary to provide an effective defence for the country and represented one of the biggest continuing burdens that today's and tomorrow's Russia will have to bear. Thus among the first measures which were supposed to cut Russia from its communist past, and help the struggling economy, was the demolition of the MIC, or at least of that particular part which happened to be in Russia. The Gaidar government, through demolition of the MIC, also wanted to show the Western democracies that Russia had totally changed and no longer represented any military threat to the West.

In 1991 Gaidar's government slashed military orders by 32 per cent and by a further 68 per cent in 1992 compared with the previous year (Mikheyev, 1996:135). By the end of 1994 military orders had dropped to 10–12 per cent of total industrial production (*ibid.*). The proportion of the defence budget in the Russian GDP fell from at least 30–35 per cent in 1991 to only 4 per cent in 1997. The production of all weapons was reduced by a factor of six and the production of certain weapons (such as chemical weapons, strategic bombers and tactical nuclear warheads) was stopped altogether (*op. cit.*:138).

Parallel with cuts in the defence budget, the Russian government stopped selling Russian weapons to traditional clients of the former Soviet Union in the developing countries. Arms sales dropped from US$11 billion in 1989 to less than US$2 billion in 1993 (*ibid.*). These cuts in defence expenditure and production affected the Russian regions in proportion to their previous involvement in the MIC.

BARRIKADY: A MILITARY ENTERPRISE

For our case study we have chosen Barrikady, a well-known military enterprise in Volgograd oblast. The enterprise's problems make it typical for provincial Russian defence enterprises.

After the Russian defeat in the war with Japan (1904–5), the Tsarist government decided to increase the country's military potential. Among the measures which were supposed to make the imperial forces stronger militarily was the construction of a gun-manufacturing plant in Tsaritsyn (later Volgograd). The tender to build such a plant attracted Russian companies as well as many foreigners. Among them there were such well-known international companies as Armstrong-Vickers, Westinghouse, De Laval, Bergmann, Oerlikon and others. In making its decision Russia used a principle which later, in Soviet times, became dominant in defence industries: 'manufacturing plant must be of a superior quality no matter what the cost'.

The tender was won by the British arms manufacturing company Armstrong-Vickers. Armstrong-Vickers was the only company which at that time was capable of producing guns of large calibre using chromium-nickel steel. The results were considered superb (Barrikady, 1989:14–15). Vickers was granted overall technical control of the project. The data deriving from the results of topographic investigations and soil analysis, together with the detailed plan of the district, were completed by Russian specialists led by the famous engineer Lieutenant-Colonel Nikolai Medinskij. Based on these data the general plan of the plant was elaborated in Sheffield where Vickers' headquarters were located.

Armstrong-Vickers assisted the Russians in finding other companies which could be engaged to provide necessary expertise. For instance, a UK-based company was invited to make drafts of buildings for the tempering shop, while a Swedish company was subcontracted to construct the brick-making factory for the plant.

Russian companies were also heavily involved in the plant construction. However, the overall management control was entirely in the hands of the British. According to the contract the British company had to provide technical support to the plant for 15 years after completion. As for payment the British company had to receive 3 million gold roubles after the plant became operational and then for the next 15 years Vickers were to receive 10 per cent of profits and 17.5 per cent of any profits exceeding 10 per cent. The plant was named Tsaritsyn Armour Plant (Tsaritcinskij Oruzhejnij Zavod) and started to manufacture large-calibre (from 5 to 16 inches) guns for the Russian navy. After the Bolshevik Revolution, as in the case of most of the country's private property, the Plant was nationalized. In 1923 it was renamed Barrikady.

The role which Barrikady played in the military industrial complex of the Soviet Union was substantial. Much unique armour has been produced there. From the 1930s the plant produced 155-mm long-range guns (BR-2) with a firing range of 25.7 km; 230-mm howitzers (B-4) with a firing range up to 18 km; 280-mm mortars (BP-18) with 16.5 km range; 460-mm guns (B-37) for waterside defence and the battleship *Soviet Union* using 1105-kg shells, with a firing range of 44.5 km; 305-mm guns (TP-52) for use in the forts in Kronshtadt, Sebastopol and Peter the Great Bay.

However, as with most of the manufacturers of armaments, the plant also produced civilian goods. In the period 1950–60 Barrikady made earth-moving equipment and the bodies of nuclear reactors for the first nuclear icebreaker *Lenin*. Rotor systems for turbo-generators of 50,000, 100,000, 200,000 and 500,000 kW capacity for the chemical and oil industries were also manufactured there.

In the 1970s, for the first time in Russia, a complex system of underwater estuary equipment (called Poisk) for floating oil rigs was designed and manufactured, which ended the US monopoly of this kind of technology. Nowadays most rigs in the Caspian Sea and Russian northern and eastern coastal waters are equipped with the boring machinery made at Barrikady. In fact, although most of the local people knew that the plant was producing mainly military, top-secret products, Barrikady was known as, and referred to in the press as, a manufacturer of oil-boring equipment.

However, the manufacture of artillery armaments was until recently the major production activity of the plant. Recent production included mobile guns such as howitzers (Msta-B) with a range of 24.5 km. Barrikady also produced parts for self-propelled howitzers, surprisingly named after flowers, such as Gvozdika (carnation), Akacia (acacia), Tulpan (tulip) and Pion (peony). Together with one of the major Russian defence enterprises in Ekaterinburg, Uraltransmach, the serial production of the advanced artillery setting Msta-C is continuing. Barrikady also developed and produced the prototype of a unique mobile artillery system called Bereg, which is aimed at beating off attacks from the sea and destroying enemy vessels located beyond the horizon line. Some interest has already been expressed in this system by states with a long coastline.

In cooperation with the R&D laboratory in Kolomna, Barrikady created the tactical rocket systems Luna (Moon), Tochka (Point), Point-U and Oka. In the 1980s the plant successfully fulfilled an urgent state order to produce mobile strategic rocket systems (Pioneer and Polar). The development of these systems, according to the Soviet press at that time, greatly improved Soviet bargaining power during the disarmament negotiations with the US. Barrikady is also involved in the Russian space programmes. In fact some components of Buran – the Russian equivalent of the space shuttle – were manufactured at the plant.

Two new Russian underground ballistic missiles (Topol-M, known in the West as the SS-X27) were positioned on 25 December 1997 in Saratov oblast close to Volgograd. These missiles were also produced by Barrikady. Interestingly, the exact location of these missiles was for the first time revealed in the Russian newspapers. Disclosure of the exact rocket sites is part of the SALT-2 agreement between the US and Russia. The new generation of ballistic missiles such as Topol-M are intended to replace missiles built in the 1970s and 1980s, the ageing PS-20 (known in the West as SS18), PC-18 (SS-19) and PC-16 (SS-17). According to some estimations Russia will need 27 ballistic missiles of the class Topol-M by the year 2008. This means that production of these missiles has to be at least two missiles a year. For Barrikady this means large state orders which could substantially improve the company's long-term prospects. However, considering the state of the Russian economy and the defence budget, the realization of these orders at present looks unlikely.

OWNERSHIP ISSUES

The initial intentions of the reformers regarding privatization were to treat defence enterprises in the same way as the rest of Russian industry. In charge of the process of privatization was the State Committee for the Management of State Property (Goskomimush-chestvo or GKI). Later, however, facing strong resistance from the military industrial lobby, privatizers made some compromises. Probably two concessions had the most significant impact on the restructuring of the defence sector. The first was that large military enterprises were allowed to remain as integrated organizations and could not be split into smaller units, which would have later allowed much more efficient restructuring. The rationale was based on the military directors' arguments that the break-up of their enterprises would undermine their production capacities and as a result would weaken Russian defence. As a consequence many of the large military enterprises are still run by the same former managements, which makes any kind of changes quite problematic. The second concession was that some major defence enterprises, in fact about 500, with all their technological links, had to be excluded altogether from the privatization process.

Barrikady found itself in this latter group. According to the authors' observations the attitudes of the top management of the enterprise, and those of some middle managers, are quite different. If the first group seems to be content with the fact that they still have the same old powers and patterns of authority, the second group seems disappointed because they have been deprived of a chance to break away from the 'dinosaur' and start running independent businesses, using the company's workshops.

PRODUCTION AND CONVERSION ISSUES

Before 1992 the ratio of military to civilian products at Barrikady was 75:25. According to the conversion programme this ratio has to be reversed by the year 2000. The initial optimism that the process of reprogramming the defence enterprises for the production of civilian goods would be a relatively easy task soon evaporated. The problems of conversion have turned out to be much more complicated. The availability of good-quality human and physical resources used for the production of top-class weaponry is no guarantee that they can be easily converted into production of civilian goods. Military production was very specific, producing specific products which often lacked equivalent civilian ones. To reorientate the production line and technology from defence products, to find new suppliers and to retrain people, requires, according to the approximate estimates made by the enterprise itself, about US$195 million, and the reorientation process would last at least 5 years.

The defence enterprises had an exclusive position in the former USSR, receiving the best of everything. However, the situation has since dramatically changed. In fact since 1992 when the defence budget was slashed by two-thirds, there has been no new investment at all at Barrikady. Much of the technological equipment is very old. In fact there is no equipment less than 5 years old, only 2.5 per cent of the equipment is 5–10 years old, 7 per cent is 10–15 years old, and the vast majority has been in use for more than 20 years.

However, the problem is in fact even more complicated. What might be important is not what Barrikady is able to produce (and the quality of the new civilian goods may be very good), but whether there will be a demand for these goods in the market place. To predict that, considering the underdevelopment of the Russian market, is a very difficult task, which none of the interviewees found it easy to appreciate.

At the moment Barrikady has developed programmes for producing coal-mining equipment, wind-powered plants producing electrical energy for smaller agricultural units, and felling machines for forestry systems. However, without additional funds these projects will not progress beyond the prototype stage.

One of the potentially large sources of finance for Barrikady's conversion programme could be the export of military goods which are still being produced. Some of these products can easily compete on world markets. However, Barrikady, as well as other defence enterprises, are not allowed to do business with foreign partners directly. Everything has to go through a giant state monopoly called 'Russian arms' or ('Rossvooruzhenie'), which controls 97 per cent of all Russian armaments. The remaining 3 per cent is divided between the official organizations 'Promexport' (Industrial export) and 'Rossijskie technologii' (Russian technologies).

To give an indication of these problems, in 1997 the Egyptian government was ready to purchase, for US$100 million, five 130-mm Bereg self-propelled coastal artillery systems. However, according to one of Barrikady's top managers, the approach was not disclosed to the enterprise because of bureaucratic inflexibility and internal political agendas.

During military exhibitions in Abu Dhabi in 1997 one of the Gulf states expressed an interest in purchasing some of the enterprise's military products, but the management of Barrikady is concerned that the deal might fall through because of the level of commission charged by Rossvooruzhenie, which would substantially increase the final price and make it less attractive to the foreign buyer. However, the management of Barrikady believes that there is still potential for entering markets such as China and India, countries keen to purchase surface-to-air missile systems, which are also developed and produced at the enterprise. At the moment the world arms market is estimated to total US$41 billion. Russia's share of this market is relatively modest at US$2.6 billion and this fact gives Barrikady's administration some hope that they can increase their sales of arms.

FINANCE

As everywhere in Russia mutual indebtedness is a critical issue at Barrikady. Retaining the status of state-owned enterprise has brought neither hoped-for security nor funds. The breakdown of the centrally planned economy with its centrally allocated suppliers and distributors, the collapse of the Soviet Union, COMECON disintegration – these are the common problems found everywhere in the Russian economy. The absence of liquidity forced Russian enterprises, including defence, to find a way to produce goods without money. Mutual arrears was the survival strategy used as much by Barrikady as the rest of the post-Soviet economy. Surprisingly the authors could not obtain actual figures regarding the mutual indebtedness as they did in other cases involving civilian enterprises. The refusal was justified by the fact that Barrikady is a defence enterprise and this information, once disclosed, could weaken its position. However, the figure of 3 billion roubles as the enterprise debt was later disclosed in one of the oblast publications.

Some interviewees expressed concern that the retention of state ownership had not secured state orders as had been expected. Even for orders obtained from the Ministry of Defence the enterprise often did not receive payment. In fact, this was happening because 'it was possible for the Ministry of Defense to keep ordering weapons in excess of what the payer, the Ministry of Finance, had been authorized to pay for' (Gaddy, 1996:94).

Another problem which makes the financial situation critical is the enterprise's inability to pay the numerous taxes it is obliged to pay. The situation at Barrikady is closely monitored by the tax office, and as soon as money comes into the enterprise it is seized by tax inspectors. The latest 'incident' happened at the end of 1997. A well-known Dutch company wanted to purchase equipment for a metallurgical plant and, in accordance with the signed contract, transferred 10 per cent as a deposit. However, the money was seized by the tax authorities and was used to pay a part of the enterprise's debt to the state budget. Another payment of 20 billion roubles from China for a fulfilled order is at the moment in the St Petersburg branch of a Russian bank. For the very same reason the company has not been able for several months to transfer the money into its account.

LABOUR

At the beginning of the reforms in 1992 Barrikady had 25,000 employees, 6 years later the number has shrunk to 7500. According to the company's HR manager the redundancies as such were not an issue. People were already leaving the enterprise voluntarily. Because they worked in the defence sector, workers were used to having better salaries, better recreational facilities and higher status than the average worker.

However, after the reforms they found themselves facing the same problems as everybody else around them. The average delay in the payment of wages was 6–8 months, salaries shrank from higher than average to lower than average in the economy; there was a loss of social facilities and a general instability. All these factors explain the drastic outflowing of labour. At the time of writing (May 1998) employees had not been paid any money since December 1997 and workers were receiving part of their wages in kind: for example in the form of food from the enterprise store and clothes and shoes through the Veteran city store.

Official statistics had already indicated in 1995 that the average monthly wage in defence enterprises was more than 60 per cent lower than in the Russian economy in general. By the end of 1997 employment in the defence sector had fallen to less than half of what it had been 10 years earlier.

It has became common practice, during the time when there are no orders and no work, that part of the labour force is sent 'on vacation' on two-thirds of the salary. All this, obviously, does not create a healthy working environment, nor does it improve discipline. According to some managers who have been with the enterprise for

20 and more years the level of working morale and discipline is the lowest in their memory. As one of them mentioned: 'People are very frustrated. They live constantly in a pre-striking state.'

Women represent a substantial proportion of employees leaving the company. An additional factor which affects their decision to leave is the irregularity of child subsidies, traditionally paid by the enterprise. In Spring 1998 there were 1500 female employees who had not received these benefits for 5 months.

The management is trying to develop a method by which to retain the remaining labour force. According to the enterprise's General Director 'the core and the best' are staying at the enterprise. The quality of labour at the defence enterprises used to be on average better than in civilian industries. In spite of the fact that there are no statistics, available information allows us to conclude that many employees who leave manage to find new employment relatively quickly. Others have moved into their own small businesses. Among the remaining workforce there are many labour dynasties, descendants of those who were among the first workers of the company in 1913–14. For them to leave the enterprise represents a personal tragedy.

There is no longer any new recruitment at Barrikady. According to staffing policy all promotions and personnel changes have to be achieved internally. While the number of production workers has declined substantially, the number of administrative personnel (although slightly reduced) remains basically the same, mostly due to the creation of new departments such as marketing and distribution.

SOCIAL INFRASTRUCTURE

As described by one of the senior managers, 'the social sphere is in total collapse'. In the past, to work in the defence industry meant getting an apartment was far easier than in most of the civilian sectors. In fact social benefits were the most attractive feature of the military enterprises, outweighing negative factors such as tougher discipline, inability to go abroad even on organized tours, to say nothing of not being permitted to travel individually. This applied even to travel to the fraternal countries of the socialist camp.

Now there is no new housing construction by the enterprise. Many social facilities are for sale, for example the Café 'Lukomorie' and the Yuri Gagarin Palace of Culture. The large Lenin Hospital, the pioneer camp on the River Volga and the sanatorium are also for sale. Actually, 'sale' is not really the right word: there is little hope of finding a cash buyer. At best the enterprise hopes to shift the responsibility for these social facilities (social'nye objekty) on to the municipal authorities. For local city leaders to take on these facilities, even free of charge, would only mean another headache, as buildings have to be maintained, employees paid, etc.

The situation at Barrikady, no matter how grim, sounds much better when it is compared to the situation of other military enterprises in the oblast. There was recently an appeal to the local government from workers at one of the companies which is well known for the excellence of its electronic products. The appeal from workers at Achtuba was published in the local newspaper *Deloviye vesti* on 24 November 1997. Workers at Achtuba who had not been paid for two years pleaded: 'We live in poverty. There is nothing to eat.... Our children complain of having headaches, fatigue. The level of haemoglobin in their blood is lower than it should be, which makes them prone to all kinds of illnesses. We cannot afford to buy school textbooks. There is no money to pay for school lunches and school security. Children have got nothing to wear. We also wear clothes bought during Brezhnev's time.'

THE MAJOR PROBLEMS AS SEEN BY THE SENIOR MANAGEMENT

According to the top management of Barrikady the major problems faced by the enterprise are: huge indebtedness (3 billion roubles in April 1998); absence of working capital; large volume of receivables; and absence of funds promised by the Federal government to finance conversion.

However, the management believes that the enterprise has a good chance of overcoming the crisis by utilizing its vast human capital and unique technology. Among the factors which have prevented the enterprise from doing so are the following:

- inefficient and suppressive tax system: according to the enterprise's financial department, for each 100 roubles of salary the enterprise has to pay 128 roubles in taxes and other payments to the state;

- monopolistic prices, uncontrolled by the Federal government, mostly for energy;

- failure of the Federal government to finance the conversion programmes;

- the combination of continuing high inflation in the country and long production cycles (up to 1 year);

- lack of financial discipline on the part of customers.

The management of Barrikady believes that the solution to their problems lies in a change of policy of the Federal government towards military enterprises undergoing conversion. Managers realize that, in order to put pressure on Moscow, they themselves are not enough. The oblast administration, together with the oblast Duma, could be much more effective in putting pressure on the Federal government. In principle, support from the Volgograd oblast administration has been granted, with a promise to help in getting a credit requested by the enterprise from the Federal budget for up to 5 years. The oblast administration also has been approached to help in paying off the debt of 3 billion roubles. Furthermore, assistance from the oblast administration could also come in the form of orders to manufacture the metal structures for a planned new bridge across the Volga River.

The city and oblast administrations realize fully that the deteriorating situation in the defence enterprises has to be addressed. On the one hand there is a large human and technological potential which could greatly contribute to oblast development. On the other hand there is the danger of a social explosion. In fact it came as no surprise when 1998 was declared as the year of conversion.

Five years earlier, in 1993, the oblast conversion programme had been developed by oblast politicians and the directors of the defence enterprises. The programme, however, did not look any different from similar documents prepared by bureaucrats of the past. The programme contained much wishful thinking and many broad and sweeping phrases. In the financial part of the programme there is an estimate of the amount of investment required to convert defence enterprises of the oblast to civilian production: US$1 billion is quoted as needed for the period up to the year 2000. It is not at all clear how this enormous amount of money is supposed to be raised. However, foreign investors are mentioned as a potential source of financing.

Considering that the inflow of all foreign direct investment into Russia in 1997 was about US$7 billion, to presume and expect that a largely unknown area will receive US$1 billion is not very realistic, to say the least.

Barrikady has recently submitted an application to achieve the status of a 'zone of economic development'. The advantage, as described in Chapter 2, may be that this status will raise the probability of attracting investors, as they will be entitled to enjoy a local tax holiday for at least 10 years. Nevertheless, outside investment is in no way guaranteed, and the future for Barrikady and other former military enterprises will continue to offer major uncertainty.

6 Milking Post-Communism

Following our exploration of the situation of industrial enterprises, this chapter reviews the transformation and development of companies involved in the production of consumer goods in Volgograd and its oblast, with particular reference to companies exploiting the region's agricultural resources.

Agriculture plays a significant role in the economy of Volgograd oblast (Barnes and Sansome, 1996). Almost 20 per cent of the economically active population are involved in agriculture. The oblast produces a range of products including cereals and maize (which are especially concentrated in the north-west of the oblast), vegetables such as tomatoes, water melons, sunflower and mustard seeds, meat (for example, pigs and poultry) and dairy products. A food-processing industry draws on these raw materials to produce a variety of meat, dairy and oil products although investment is deemed necessary to exploit more effectively and develop areas such as the production of tomato paste and sunflower oil. The oblast has 13 meat and 34 dairy kombinats producing a limited range of meat and dairy products.

The pace of agricultural reforms has been slow. The agricultural sector is inherently conservative. The disappearance of central government credits for agricultural enterprises has been accompanied by a major decline in regional investment in agriculture. Not surprisingly this has resulted in an overall decline in agricultural output.

At the same time the chapter also explores the changing situation of consumers, company responses to the establishment of liberalized markets for consumer goods and the resulting impact on retailing and the retailing structure in the area. Under communism neither private consumers nor the enterprises catering for their needs enjoyed high priority. At best one could argue that successive governments sought to meet the basic needs of the population. Centralized control of production and distribution resulted in widespread, endemic shortages so that queues and queueing (as an everyday activity) were engrained features of Soviet life. Consumer goods were in general distributed through state-owned department stores and 'generic' retail outlets which supplied a standard range of goods.

The collapse of the communist system and the decision to establish a market economy have brought about a marked transformation in the range of goods and the means of their distribution. Small privatization and the possibilities offered to individuals to set up their own businesses, as well as the entry into the market of foreign goods and companies, have created a variegated range of goods, suppliers and retailers. The shortages of the former system have given way to considerable choice and competition.

The changes in the supply of consumer goods manifest themselves in a number of ways:

• There is now a considerable range of retail 'outlets', from smallholders and pensioners selling farm produce on the street out of buckets and boxes to the ubiquitous kiosks selling tobacco products and alcoholic beverages, to market stalls as well as more traditional shops. The former main department store in the city centre has become a collection of independent 'boutiques' selling all manner of domestic and household items, both practical and for leisure. Where people once queued in the expectation of finding something to buy, people now go to view and compare (possibly also wondering whether they can afford what is on display). At the top of the range there are 'exclusive' shops selling expensive products such as designer clothing.

• The range and variety of products have expanded enormously. The open-air market in the Traktornij district has a predominance of stalls selling fur and leather garments. A confectionery retailer located in one of the main streets of the centre offers an extensive range of chocolate, pralines and other sweets. This variety is also evident in cafés and restaurants which vary from the most basic (redolent literally of the Soviet era) to pavement cafés and exclusive and expensive restaurants.

• The products on sale comprise the output of both domestic and foreign producers. The increasing internationalization of the goods on offer is evident from the presence of Western brands (although not all are necessarily genuine). Western products have penetrated many areas of retailing including food and drinks, clothing, white goods and motor vehicles. In general, the collapse of former systems of state support has been to the detriment of domestic enterprises. The fur coats at the Traktornij district market would previously have been made up in the Soviet Union. The abolition of low-interest credits which enabled domestic manufacturers to acquire the pelts has opened the door to foreign companies (many from Greece and Turkey). These foreign companies now buy the pelts, have them made into coats and hats on their own territory and then re-export these to Russia for sale on local markets.

Many outlets offer both domestic and foreign products for sale. It is not unusual for consumers to be able to choose between a range of foreign and domestic beers or even yoghurts. Initially (that is, on the collapse of communism) domestic goods may have been regarded as inferior to foreign products by many consumers. Many domestic companies, however, have raised the quality of their products and their presentation so that consumers can choose on the basis of taste as well as on quality and price. Consequently domestic products are no longer necessarily regarded as inferior to imports.

- Competition between outlets is substantial because of the considerable variety and choice available. Supply of consumer goods is no longer a problem – choosing and affording have, however, become critical issues for large sections of the population as a result of unemployment, low wages, non-payment of wages, etc.

CONSUMER GOODS PRODUCTION

In the command economy, enterprises producing consumer goods were given workmanlike names such as Meat Factory No. 1 and Milk Factory No. 3 (compare these names to those given to the military establishments, the steel works and the tractor plant).

In Volgograd there had been a number of plants taking agricultural products such as meat and milk from the region and processing them for generally local consumption. These enterprises clearly fulfilled an important function in supplying the population with foodstuffs. However, they lacked the charisma which the official ideology afforded to steel plants and other enterprises in the sector of heavy industry and military production.

With the dismantlement of the command economy a very small proportion of such enterprises was acquired by, or attracted investment, from foreign companies. For example, the brewery in Volzhsky now also produces and distributes Coca Cola. Greek and Italian investors have acquired an interest in pig-breeding establishments.

However, both nationally and locally, foreign direct investment has been relatively low. The food-processing plants in the Volgograd region have therefore been largely left to their own devices to adapt to the new circumstances. Volgograd had two major food-processing companies in 1997: the Meat Factory and Milk Factory No. 1. The next section of this chapter explores the development of Milk Factory No. 1 since 1992.

MILK FACTORY No. 1

Milk Factory No. 1 is one of around 30 milk-processing plants in Volgograd oblast and the leading such plant in Volgograd city. Originally one of three milk factories in the city, Milk Factory No. 1 now has a dominant position – Milk Factory No. 2 went bankrupt and Milk Factory No. 3 is experiencing considerable difficulties. Milk Factory No. 1 became a joint-stock company in 1992. The company's shareholders comprise 450 individual shareholders and 24 legal entities (in general cooperative farmers supplying milk to the factory). Initially 51 per cent of the company's shares were held by internal shareholders, with the remainder in the hands of input suppliers. A subsequent share issue resulted in a dilution of share ownership, with only 35 per cent of shares being held by internal shareholders, who as a group are controlled by the company's management team.

The situation for companies in Volgograd oblast such as Milk Factory No. 1 contrasts greatly with the situation prevailing in nearby Ulianovsk oblast where only six out of 24 milk factories are profitable. One explanation for the different conditions is that the administration in Ulianovsk oblast controls the prices for milk products so that, according to local producers, their activities are driven by the decision of the provincial bureaucracy rather than by the market. One consequence of this situation was that in 1997 butter, as under the previous regime, was distributed to the local population on the basis of coupons (i.e. butter was still being rationed).

STRUCTURE

The company's main plant and headquarters are close to Volgograd city centre, although the company has also built two smaller plants in the suburbs.

In addition to maintaining and developing its milk-processing capability the company has expanded into retailing and now owns a supermarket and 10 shops in the city. It supplies a further 300 shops in Volgograd. The company also carries out much of its own transportation.

Milk Factory No. 1 has its own training centre which offers courses in business and technology to its employees. Furthermore, it has established links with a number of academic research institutes.

A key relationship is with the company's suppliers as the quality of the milk is paramount for production and the managing director readily recognizes that 'good-quality supplies are one reason for our success'. The company for its part selects its suppliers carefully and has contracts with specific farms which are situated at a distance of from 40 to 250 km from Volgograd.

In total Milk Factory No. 1 has approximately 650 employees, of whom 400 work in the processing plants and 250 in the retail outlets.

PRODUCTS AND MARKETS

The company basically processes 'raw' milk into a range of milk-based products which, in addition to milk itself, include yoghurt, soft cheese and kefir. In fact the company could in 1997 make the entire range of milk products except hard cheese. The period since 1992 has been marked by a significant increase in the range of products offered by the company and 30 new products have been added to the range. It now sells over 60 different products.

Product development has been (and continues to be) an important component of the company's strategy. The expansion of the product range achieved so far has enabled the company to offer consumers greater choice. Planned developments include the production of hard cheese and a greater emphasis on so-called health products, for example, products containing vitamins and amino acids as well as live yoghurts; products for the growing number of vegetarians; and products for children. The last-mentioned group of products are considered particularly attractive as the government gives tax breaks on the profits derived from sales of children's products. Product development goes hand in hand with a two-strand marketing strategy of enhancing product appearance (i.e. packaging) and consolidating the company's presence in the marketplace. There has been a rapid transition from offering 'generic' products (milk, kefir) in unsophisticated containers to branded products presented in a way to attract consumers' attention.

The overall strategic aim has been to maximize the company's market share. The company is present throughout Volgograd oblast as well as in the neighbouring Rostov and Voronezh regions. As previously mentioned, the company distributes its products through its own supermarket and shops as well as through 300 shops in Volgograd. This gives the company a substantial presence in the local market. Additionally it supplies milk to schools and kindergartens which together take one-third of the company's milk production.

Compared to the past, the First Milk Company, as it now presents itself, has a strong marketing orientation and has identified key markets and segments for its products. The company monitors sales closely and uses its retail outlets as barometers of consumer demand. As the managing director proudly stated: 'Milkmen adapted to capitalism more quickly than everyone else!'

QUALITY AND STANDARDS

The company has undertaken considerable investment in upgrading the quality of products and the production process and in reducing costs. The managing director aims to 'do today what others will think about tomorrow'. The company has set up new processing plants in suburban areas of Volgograd and has modernized the production facilities on its main site. New equipment has included packaging equipment which the company purchased. Originally the company had leased the equipment from a major multi-national company but had found the cost of buying the necessary inputs exorbitant.

The company is keen to produce products in such a way that the environment is not damaged. Within the company there is a department which is responsible for the quality of inputs and for standards. The work of this department is complemented by other activities. The company is working to achieve ISO 9000 certification and is working with the German Standards Agency TÜV and Lloyds on this. This involves a 14-month programme focusing on quality and costs.

The company has also established contacts with a number of research institutes which are assisting the company to develop products which are not detrimental to the environment. The company aims to achieve the internationally recognized environmental standard ISO 14000 and has involved around a dozen research institutes in this project.

A further activity relates to the development of the company's own employees and also its suppliers. The company set up its own training centre in 1992. Since then the centre has been running courses for employees to increase their commercial and technical expertise. As well as developing its employees in areas relating to the ecological impact of production, the company has involved its suppliers in this process, in order to raise their awareness of the environmental issues related to milk production.

COMPETITION

The First Milk Company is a strong player in its markets. Competition is constrained in part by the practicalities of transporting milk (and milk products) over long distances. The company's products compete with those from local and other competitors such as Volgograd's Milk Factory No. 3, the Volzhsky Milk Factory, the Russian Milk and Meat Company and foreign companies whose products are transported over long distances to reach Volgograd.

Some smaller retailers complain that the company restricts the distribution of its products, preventing some retailers from selling the company's products and favouring certain outlets. The company's strategy, however, is not based on undercutting competitors' prices as the price of the company's products will be sometimes dearer, sometimes cheaper than those of competitors, both domestic and foreign.

VERTICAL INTEGRATION

A conspicuous feature of the company's strategy has been vertical integration, particularly, but not exclusively, through expansion into retailing. The company has a strong hold on the totality of the supply chain, from the supply of key raw materials such as milk to distribution and retailing. Suppliers are 'tied in' to the company through supply contracts and in some cases as shareholders of the company. In this way the company seeks to secure an appropriate supply of milk of the right quality. With regard to distribution the company uses a combination of company and independent lorry drivers. It is, however, the company's intention to bring the distribution system totally in house.

The most obvious manifestation of vertical integration has been the company's expansion into retailing. This aspect of the company's activity comprises one supermarket and 10 shops. The shops sell not only the company's products but a broad range of foods. One of the shops specializes in products for babies, and sells baby foods as well as other products for infants. Sales of the company's products through its own shops have increased from 20 per cent of production in 1996 to 30 per cent in 1997. The aim is to increase this percentage even more.

The retail activity is regarded as a dimension of the company's overall marketing activity (complementing the advertising conducted in the media – television, radio and press). First, the managing director regards the company's shops as the company's most effective marketing instrument. Second, the company sees its shops as sites for market research, permitting it to monitor directly what consumers are purchasing and to facilitate the company's response to consumer demand.

Third, the retail outlets are sources of cash (the managing director describes them as the company's 'cash cows') and account for one-quarter of overall sales. In fact the outlets are estimated to earn more than 100 million roubles a day (*Delovoy Povolzhie*, no. 25, 1997:3). In the general climate of inter-company indebtedness access to cash is a major problem facing Russian companies. This problem can be alleviated, at least in part, by involvement in retailing activities. A further argument for ownership of retail outlets is that smaller retailers are not able to sell the company's products properly and are frequently unable to pay for them.

Smaller retailers, especially those denied access to the company's products, complain that the First Milk Factory is in fact abusing its market position and is squeezing them on two fronts – refusing to supply them with its products and offering unfair competition to their own retailing activities.

Questions have also been raised with regard to the company's strategy for its shops. When the shops are established, they are given profit targets. As soon as the shops achieve certain standards and performance targets (for example, profitability), they are divested. Questions have been raised about the appropriateness of such a policy and its congruence with the company's overall strategy. Furthermore, concerns have been expressed about the nature of the sale of retail outlets and the beneficiaries.

Such concerns are expressed about many of the larger companies involved in the production of consumer goods. A number of food manufacturers have become involved in retailing, directly affecting the price of goods and restricting their supply. These companies justify these activities by the inability of other retailers to sell their products effectively and to pay the companies for them. Expansion in retailing is often at the expense of upgrading production, which in many cases is sorely needed. It is also not always clear how companies, burdened with debt, can finance such expansion (either through acquisition or leasing of retail outlets). The shops themselves do not necessarily become profitable, but are still sold off to 'insiders' at knock-down prices in spite of the substantial amounts of company money invested in them.

FUTURE PLANS AT THE FIRST MILK FACTORY

The First Milk Factory has established a strong market position in Volgograd. It is considered a good employer. Only once in its history did the company delay in paying wages – by 10 days – when it was paying for new equipment it had purchased. New employment opportunities within the company are limited and the company resists pressure from the city administration to take on more workers.

The attainment of international standards such as ISO 9000 and ISO 14000 will help to upgrade the company's processes and strengthen its ability to compete with domestic and foreign competitors. The company intends to expand into other regions of Russia.

Product development will also continue and the company profiles itself as a manufacturer of health products. In the short term the company is planning to acquire machinery that will enable it to produce yoghurt in 25 g containers. The benefit of this for the company is that it will be able to produce yoghurts without preservatives.

The company also intends to bring distribution fully under its control. Transport logistics have already been computerized and the company would like to bring all of the transportation activities in house.

Finally, the managing director wishes to re-establish actual majority control of the company's shares by the internal shareholders in order to achieve greater security and control and to eliminate the possibility of interference or take-over by parties external to the company.

CONCLUSION

A number of general points can be drawn from an analysis of the First Milk Company in the context of the evolving market conditions in Volgograd and its oblast. First, marketization has created a highly fragmented structure in the agricultural sector and in retailing. The formerly centralized organization of production and retailing has given way to an atomized structure of producing and retailing companies and to increasing competition. In such a situation there are few substantial players. These circumstances, moreover, provide opportunities for companies such as the First Milk Company, with a developed strategy and the necessary resources, to secure a significant position within the marketplace.

Second, marketization has, perhaps paradoxically, encouraged a process of monopolization. Many interviewees expressed a desire for the benefits of open markets but at the same time wanted protection (from the local administration or the federal authorities) to help them resist what they considered to be excessive or unfair competitive pressures. The First Milk Company's strategy has been clearly predicated on vertical integration, controlling the overall chain of economic activities from the supply of raw materials, to production, distribution and retailing. This strategy has been facilitated by low supplier power and the fragmented nature of the retail sector. The company can be considered as being able to exert greater market power than either its suppliers or its purchasers (both consumers and other retailers wanting to sell the company's products).

The strategy of vertical integration has been developed in parallel with a policy of autarky, of doing as much as possible in house. Autarky was a typical feature of the command economy and its persistence is manifested in the company's aim to bring distribution totally within its control. Autarky thus complements vertical integration by raising the company's ability to control necessary resources, reducing its reliance on external market factors.

Third, the company's expansion into retailing can be explained in three ways. Retailing represents the logical culmination of the policy of vertical integration, ensuring that the company's products are brought to the end-users. The company therefore does not need to compete so intensively with other suppliers for a presence in the retail outlets. Furthermore, retailing is attractive as a source of cash generation as ordinary consumers have no choice but to pay cash for the company's products.

There is also perhaps a more sinister interpretation relating to the establishment and divestment of retail outlets. The company is clearly investing resources in setting up and developing retail outlets. What is the underlying rationale for subsequently selling off these outlets? Why sell them off at all if they play a significant part in the policy of vertical integration and as 'cash cows'? One argument could be that divestment results in a substantial cash injection for the company which recoups the investment disbursed to set up and develop the outlet. In Russia's current economic climate, however, there are widespread rumours (and facts) regarding the misappropriation of company property to the benefit of particular individuals.

Fourth, reflecting the aims of vertical integration and autarky, there is a clear aim within the top management of the company to retain and reinforce insider control, thus further saving the company from the influence of external forces and pressures. Taken together insider control, vertical integration and autarky seek to limit the company's exposure to external and potentially destructive forces. It is almost as if the company wishes to re-create the certainties of the former system. At a different level, this constellation of factors gives those who control the company's resources greater discretion to dispose of the company's resources as they see fit, relatively unencumbered by 'market' controls (although this does not prevent, it even encourages, rumours and gossip). The interest of the collective is seen to have given way to the interests of a restricted group of insiders.

It is difficult to say why the First Milk Factory rather than any other of its local competitors should have been so successful. Clearly a number of factors – including its condition at the onset of market reforms, the quality, vision and ambition of its top management and the demand for its products – will have played a role. However, the development of the company is not atypical in that there have been successful company transformations in the period of transition to a market economy. Interestingly the success of the First Milk Company has been based on both exploiting and creating a defence against market forces.

7 Entrepreneurs

INTRODUCTION

With the advent of Soviet communism small businesses, the so-called 'schools of entrepreneurship', were virtually destroyed. The remaining fragments were spread over into the black market sector of the economy and survived to a certain extent in agriculture. It hardly needs to be said that according to the Marxist view there is no place for private property in a communist state.

For more than 70 years state ownership was dominant in the Soviet Union, accounting for 98 per cent of all property. Selling goods made by other people and employing outside of the family were declared illegal. It is therefore not surprising that, even after the reforms in Russia, there is still resistance to and misunderstanding of small businesses.

The first part of this chapter analyses the dynamics of the development of small business in Russia in general and in Volgograd oblast in particular. The second part of the chapter, by means of case studies, attempts to give some insights into the problems faced by three entrepreneurs located in the Volgograd oblast.

TYPOLOGY OF SMALL BUSINESS IN RUSSIA

In the former USSR, according to the Law on Enterprises (1990), two criteria were used to define small business: number of employees and turnover.

However, in the resolution of the Soviet of Ministers of 18 August 1990, regarding the establishment and development of small business, the second criterion was abolished. Since that time the criterion based on the number of employees has not changed. What has changed, however, is the actual number of employees in the various branches of small business activity (Table 7.1).

One of the most important pieces of legislation regarding small business was the law 'On state support for small entrepreneurship' (1995), which widened the subjects of small business to include those entrepreneurial individuals not formally registered as small businesses. In addition this law stated that business cannot be classified as a small business if 25 per cent or more of the assets are owned by the state. The upper limit for classification as a small business was raised in a majority of branches which allowed more enterprises to qualify for the status of small business enterprise and for state support.

Table 7.1   Quantitative characteristics of small business in the USSR and later in Russia: maximum number of employees

Area of activity	From 8 August 1990	From 18 July 1991	From 14 June 1995
Retail trade	15	15	30
Municipal service	25	15	30
Wholesale trade	25	25	30
Agriculture	50	50	60
R&D	100	25	60
Construction	200	200	100
Industry	200	200	100
Transport	100	100	100

Sources: The Law 'On state support for small entrepreneurship', 1995; the resolution of the Soviet of Ministers of the USSR, no. 790, 18 August 1990.

During 1980–90 almost all small enterprises had been set up as part of state enterprises and used state property. However, as a result of the 1995 legislation, by 1996 the classification of small business based on the type of property ownership looked very different. Eighty-five per cent of small business was now based in private property, with only 15 per cent based on other forms of ownership such as on municipal property, state property and the property of civil institutions (*Ekonomika i zhizn*, 1996:17).

THE DYNAMICS OF SMALL BUSINESS DEVELOPMENT IN RUSSIA

Thirty-two per cent of all small businesses are concentrated in the Central economic region of Russia, with the core (21.1 per cent) in Moscow. Thirty per cent are situated in the North economic region, with 9.1 per cent in the north-west, and the core (7 per cent) in St Petersburg. A further 10 per cent are situated in the North-Caucasian region. The Volgograd area accounts for about 2 per cent of all Russian small businesses. There is an obvious regional imbalance (Dmitriev 1996).

In 1997 there were about 1 million registered small businesses in Russia; however, it is not known how many of these actually function. The statistics of small business are complicated by the fact that criteria, such as number of employees, have changed three times since 1991. Furthermore, small businesses have appeared as a reaction against the process of restructuring, privatization and demonopolization in Russia, as well as a consequence of founding new ones.

Table 7.2 Major indicators of the development of small business

	1991	*1992*	*1993*	*1994*	*1995*
No. of small businesses (000s)	268	560	865	1000	1000
Percentage compared with previous year	–	209	155	116	100
No. employed in small business sector (000s)	5441	7077	8630	9500	14000
Percentage compared with previous year	–	130	122	110	147

Source: Own calculations based on Dmitriev (1996).

Table 7.2 shows that the growth in the number of small businesses reached its peak in 1994 and since 1992 growth rates have been declining. However, the absolute number of people employed in the sector has been growing steadily. Most Russian researchers agree that employment in the small business sector will continue to grow and will probably reach 13–15 million people by the year 2000, with up to 2 million small businesses. If one takes into account people working in small business as their secondary business activity, then the number of small businesses could be as many as 21–30 million.

In 1997 approximately 20 per cent of the active population (including the agricultural sector) were working in the small business sector. For more than 10 million of them it was the only source of income. In the construction industry and information sector, 50 per cent of employment was due to small business, and in the trade and real-estate sectors the figure was 85–95 per cent. One of the typical features of Russian small business is that many people find their second, third or sometimes fourth job in the small business sector. In 1997 more than 5 million people were sharing their main employment with work in small enterprises. Overall 45 million people were benefiting from income from small business.

The input of small business into the Russian economy even at this stage of its transformation is quite substantial. Approximately 12 per cent of official GDP is created in the small business sector. Thirty per cent of contract work in the construction industry, 9 per cent of industrial production, and approximately 20 per cent of the retail trade is carried out by small businesses (*op. cit.*:37). However, comparison with the role of small business in more advanced economies shows that Russian small business is still underdeveloped.

SMALL BUSINESS LEGISLATION

The perestroika and especially post-perestroika period were marked by an enormous volume of legislation. New laws were adopted and, almost instantly, amended by numerous additions, Acts of Parliament and presidential decrees of different kinds until these laws often lost their initial significance and purpose. A weak legislative system, together with pressures from a vast number of different lobbying groups, produced often contradictory legislation which was frequently confusing for both professional bureaucrats and small entrepreneurs.

For instance, after the Law on Enterprises, and the Resolution of the Soviet of Ministers 'On the development of small business' (both 1990), there were also Laws 'On ownership' and 'On entrepreneurial activity' which themselves created the foundation for further legislation. Among the more recent pieces of legislation the Resolution of the Government of Russia (no. 1413, 29 December 1994), 'On networks of regional agencies of support for small businesses', stated that a network of non-state regional offices had to be created for the provision of consultancy, education, feasibility studies of small business projects, information, and assistance in submitting documents necessary for the registration of small businesses.

The Presidential Decree of 30 November 1993 envisaged privileged taxation of small businesses functioning in the industrial sphere, allocation of centralized credit to the priority areas of industrial development, creation of special funds to support small business, provision of state guarantees, and the creation of state insurance funds for these purposes.

For the implementation of this Decree a new resolution was adopted which established a fund for the support of entrepreneurship and the development of competition by the State Committee of Anti-monopoly Policy and Support for the New Economic Structures.

The Governmental Resolution of 11 May 1993 had aimed to unify different pieces of legislation into a logical document which would constitute the basis for the financial, informational, technical and educational support of small businesses, together with assistance for their international activities. The Resolution also defined priority areas for small business. These included: production and processing of agricultural goods; production of consumer goods, medical equipment and medicine; provision of communal and industrial services; construction of private houses and development of social and industrial infrastructure; innovation activities.

In addition a Law 'On state support for small entrepreneurship' (1995) outlined general guidelines for the forms and methods of state involvement in small business.

In order to support the innovative activity of small businesses a Resolution of the Government of Russia of 2 February 1994 set up a fund in support of small businesses in R&D areas. One of the more recent pieces of legislation was the Resolution of the Government of Russia of 18 December 1995 (No. 1256) which established a federal programme of state support for small businesses for the period 1996–7.

Clearly there is no lack of legislation. This indicates that the importance of small business is recognized at the very top of Russian politics, yet there is not enough information on how, where, and in what form small entrepreneurs can obtain help from the state. None of the small businesses we interviewed for our case studies knew about or believed in the possibility of getting state support. There are three major problems in the Russian legislation concerning small business which are similar to problems in the legislation in general. Firstly, there is a low rate of enforcement, which often comes as a result of good intentions but with insufficient funds for implementation. For example, Russian legislation already requires 15 per cent of state orders to be reserved for small and medium-sized enterprises (Golikova and Avilova, 1997:425). However, there is no appropriate allocation of funds for this in the federal budget. In fact, according to legislation, from 2 to 4 per cent of GDP must be allocated to support small business. In reality, however, state support is only one-tenth of this (Dmitriev, 1996:90). Secondly, there is a multiplicity of additions and amendments to the main legislation at every level of government, from regional to provincial and municipal. Often these additions contradict each other, changing the meaning of the original law or resolution. Thirdly, there is a complicated claims procedure, and also lack of clear information about the availability of support programmes and how small entrepreneurs can obtain allocated funds. For example, in 1995 a Guarantee Fund of 25 billion roubles was established to help small entrepreneurs to start and develop businesses. However, not a single rouble has been allocated due to the complicated, multi-layer claims system (Ksenofontova *et al.*, 1996, no. 6, pp. 15–20).

THE DEVELOPMENT OF SMALL BUSINESS IN VOLGOGRAD AND ITS OBLAST

Of around 40,000 enterprises situated in the oblast about 95 per cent belong to non-state enterprises and 35 per cent of these are small businesses. Table 7.3 shows the sectoral division of small business in Volgograd and its oblast at the beginning of 1997.

The majority of small businesses are in catering and trade (8739 enterprises with 60,276 employees). Three areas of small business in Volgograd and its region (trade, catering, construction and industry) account for 85 per cent of employment and constitute 80 per cent of all small businesses. The number of small businesses has increased by a multiple of more than 21 from 1991 to March 1996: from 950 in 1991 to about 20,000. However, growth is understandably slowing down. If in 1991 the number of small businesses grew 9 times compared to 1990, in 1995 the growth compared to the previous year was just 25 per cent. However, the number of people working in the small business sector grew four-fold over the same period.

The percentage of people working in small business, compared to total employment in Volgograd and its oblast, went up from 3 per cent or 30,000 in 1991 to more than 25 per cent or almost 200,000 in 1997. The contribution of small business to the oblast's GDP is still very modest, being only slightly more than 5 per cent in 1995. However, in trade small business accounts for 30 per cent of output, and in construction for 80 per cent. This dynamic is typical of the Russian economy as a whole. Interestingly the majority of small businessmen are involved in at least two or three side activities, which are often connected with mediation in trade.

Table 7.3 Sectoral division of small business in Volgograd and its oblast (January 1997)

Type of enterprise	No. of enterprises	No. of employees
Industrial	2093	40277
Agricultural	543	5474
Forestry	14	292
Transport, communication	249	2128
Construction	3822	52454
Trade and catering	8739	60276
Supply and sale	216	2318
Delivery services	59	347
Information	52	372
Real estate	751	3877
General commerce	21	158
Geological	108	905
Craft	104	2737
Physical education and health service	268	1363
Sport	671	3737
Scientific	145	1054
Financial	184	1103
Total	**18339**	**178874**

Source: Own calculation based on *Volgogradskij statisticheskij sbornik* (1997) and Dmitriev (1996).

MAJOR PROBLEMS OF SMALL BUSINESS

Lack of finances and credits

Small businesses have in general a limited financial base, and in 1997 74 per cent of entrepreneurs used their own savings as starting capital. Five per cent had to borrow from friends and relatives and only 3 per cent received financial support from the state. The number of entrepreneurs using bank credit decreased substantially, from 29 per cent of small businesses in 1992 to 19 per cent in 1997. Explaining their reluctance to approach banks, small businessmen mentioned high interest rates, a requirement to give their property as security, and a lack of long-term credits (that is, for more than 2 years). In fact it is the policy of the majority of Russian private banks not to offer credits to small businesses (Dolgov, 1993:34).

State credit lines

According to State legislation most of the requirements of small businesses for external funding must to be supported by the federal budget. The mechanics of this are relatively simple. The project proposed by a small business is firstly assessed by the Fund of Projects and Programmes (FPP). If a positive decision is made, then the selected commercial bank releases the finances, charging market interest rates. However, the small business is allocated the finances at much lower rates, with the difference covered by the federal budget. The opening of the credit line is supervised by Mezheconomsber Bank, which also acts as a guarantor for the commercial banks that actually provide the credit.

In reality it is quite complex to obtain access to this preferential credit. First, the small business has to submit a project to the local branch of the FPP. A feasibility study has to be conducted within a month of submission and then, if the project is considered suitable, the application is submitted to the federal FPP where, as a rule, lobbying is needed, for which small businesses might have neither enough time nor money. In fact this situation seems to be typical of all the regions of Russia. According to Golikova and Avilova (1997) one entrepreneur in three sees no point in submitting an application because they think that the money will go only to pre-selected firms.

The second obstacle is that, in order to receive credit, the small business has to put down a payment amounting to between 50 and 70 per cent of the total value of the project. Obviously that severely limits the number of applicants.

The third problem is that the maximum duration of the project and the repayment term is just 1–2 years (Vorochalina, 1996, 7, pp. 83–7). Clearly it is very difficult to meet such tight conditions, even with the very high rates of return in Russia.

Obsolete equipment

Most of the equipment used by small businesses is obsolete. In fact equipment represents only 3 per cent of the value of the main factors of production belonging to small businesses. Lack of financial resources does not allow small businesses to buy new equipment, or even to maintain the old. According to some estimates only 37 per cent of small businesses have computers and only 26 per cent photocopiers. However, there are also some positive signs. In 1995 there was a four-fold increase in self-financed investment, with self-investment increasing over 7 times in industry.

Structure of production

The former Soviet practice of gigantism, with the accent on big industrial production, is echoed in the absence of small equipment suitable for the small business sector. This problem is most acute in the agricultural sector, where farmers badly need special agricultural machinery and equipment for use in small-scale production.

Lack of education and retraining

The majority of small businessmen have never received any formal business education. Interestingly, it seems that the most successful of them have gained their experience while working in the black-market economy. Often they use the same old assured practices. Entrepreneurs often acknowledge the necessity for business education; however, more out of politeness than a real belief in its importance. Russian economic reality is full of examples in which success has no correlation with business education. Business education is provided mostly by private institutions, and small entrepreneurs have neither enough funds available for this purpose, nor enough time.

Lack of insurance

There is no system of insurance for small businesses. The existing insurance system cannot meet the demands of large companies, to say nothing of small businesses, where the risk rating is usually higher. There is no system in place of state guarantees for small businesses.

Tax system

The absence of a supportive and clear tax system is among the most damaging factors discriminating against small business. Although the tax on profit is 35 per cent, this is not actually the major problem for small entrepreneurs. More significant is the fact that at the beginning of 1998 there were more than 40 different taxes and obligatory payments to be met by small businesses. According to the Ministry of Finance the sum of these taxes and other payments totals 90 per cent of a company's profit. In trying to beat the system, small businesses hide their profits, as well as some of their production and services. For this purpose double accountancy systems are used: one is real, reflecting the existing state of affairs and is used for internal purposes; the other is distorted, and is given to the tax inspectors. Entrepreneurs try to increase on paper the cost of their production and the prices of inputs such as electricity and gas. It would be accurate to say that in many cases the state itself pushes small businesses towards this illegal form of behaviour. Very often the dilemma which is faced by small businesses is quite simple: to be honest and meet all the required payments and consequently go bankrupt, or to behave illegally and survive and prosper.

At the time of writing there was no difference between the requirement of provision of financial information between large enterprises and small businesses. This situation uses up valuable and limited resources of small businesses, makes their functioning more complicated and increases their overheads.

Bureaucracy and administrative barriers

Registration is costly and time-consuming, and cannot be done by post. The fastest way is the personal approach, that is, to go to different offices and collect the necessary signatures. Often knowing someone in the administration can speed up the process dramatically.

An additional problem is that state bureaucrats may (intentionally or otherwise) not explain the bureaucratic procedure correctly, and they may unlawfully reject the registration or impose an inappropriate fee. Municipal authorities can manipulate the rent of state property, reducing it in some cases and increasing it in others.

According to Russian research on small business (Dmitriev, 1996) bureaucrats extort money in two forms: semi-legal and illegal. Semi-legal practices include forcing enterprises to contribute 'voluntarily' to the needs of the city, such as street and house maintenance. In one of our case studies the firm was instructed by a senior member of the mayor's office to change the colour of the company building's facade prior to an official visit to Volgograd by the former Russian Prime Minister Chernomyrdin in August 1997. The same orders were received by telephone by all the enterprises whose premises faced the main street. A majority felt compelled to comply. Illegal forms include straightforward bribery.

Corruption and racket

Currently corruption is the most common form of illegal economic activity. As Radaev points out, 'Reforms and unclear legislation have blurred the difference between legal and illegal activity. Nowadays bribes have reached proportions that the Soviet bureaucrat could never have imagined even in his wildest dreams' (Radaev, 1994:80).

The state, in trying to fight corruption, very often actually breeds it. Most of the small business people we interviewed admitted that they do not have a clear idea who has the right to inspect their economic activity. There are so many controlling organs with unclear responsibilities and duties that they often duplicate each other, making the small entrepreneur sceptical about their intentions.

During the first years of legalization on small business activity there were numerous appalling examples of pure-form racket. However, recently there has been a shift from racket to so-called organized protection. All enterprises have to have protection, known as 'krysha' or 'roof'. There are three types of institutions which offer this kind of service: legal law enforcement agencies functioning on a commercial basis; officially registered private security companies, consisting of former policemen or KGB agents; and criminal organizations used by many small businesses. Nowadays entrepreneurs are no longer paying outside racketeers but are using their own 'security personnel'.

Another semi-legal service has made its appearance as a reaction against the inefficiency of the legal debt collection system, such as arbitration courts, which are overloaded with cases and understaffed. Professional debt collectors have become part of the business landscape of Russia. According to some sources they frequently take half of the collected debt as their fee (Radaev, 1994:78).

Impoverishment of the population (lack of effective demand)

According to official statistics approximately 30 per cent of the population still live below the poverty level (Shulus, 1996). Lack of effective demand is one of the main obstacles for the growth and development of small business.

Lack of stimuli for long-term business

According to Scase (1997) it is necessary to make a distinction between entrepreneurial activity and small-scale business proprietorship.

Typical of the first activity is long-term capital accumulation which often goes hand in hand with sacrifices in personal consumption. The second is marked by a basic desire to raise personal consumption rather than to promote business expansion. It is impossible to tell quantitatively how many entrepreneurs in Russia belong to each of these two groups. However, the lack of general economic and political stability in the country, alongside an absence of real support from the state, does not encourage small businesses to aim for long-term development. Confirmation of this can be found in the fact that only 28 per cent of the small business activity in Volgograd and its oblast requires long-term investment in capital goods. The magnitude of the problems faced by small business explains the negative dynamics of small business evolution, with many businesses surviving for less than 1 year.

According to government statistics only 5 per cent of small businesses registered in 1991 are still active in the market. If this negative trend continues, it could have a negative impact on the development of small business and on Russian transformation as a whole.

CASE STUDIES

The changes in the Russian economic structure, brought about by decentralization, commercialization and privatization, prepared the ground for the appearance of small businesses on a mass scale. The popular slogan of the end of the 1980s, 'Chto ne zaprescheno – razresheno' ('What is not forbidden – is allowed') indicated official acceptance of small business development.

Hundreds of thousands of people, generally without any entrepreneurial experience, rushed into government offices, often forming lengthy queues, in order to register their businesses. The motivation to start small businesses varied enormously. Some wanted to realize their life-long goals of being independent. Some moved into entrepreneurship because of despair after being made redundant, or not being paid for months, or being pushed into unpaid holidays due to the collapse of demand for factory products. Some took the opportunity to launder their 'dirty money'. Some expected to get rich quickly, usually naively, although a small number were highly successful.

The following case studies explore the experiences of three Volgograd entrepreneurs who, we believe, share many of the problems, aspirations and worries of millions like them all over the new Russia.

CASE STUDY ONE: MIKHAIL

Mikhail, a man in his early 30s, owns a prosperous food store, 'Aelita', in the centre of Volgograd. After graduating from a 4-year course at music college he was admitted to the Astrakhan Conservatory. However, after completing the first year he was called up to serve for 2 years in the Russian army, where he became a singer in the North Caucasian Soviet Army Ensemble. With the choir he travelled extensively around the former USSR.

He returned to Volgograd in 1988 and founded his own Cossack choir, the popularity of which grew rapidly. In Volgograd and its region there are many Cossacks who would often travel for hours to get to a concert.

In the atmosphere of the third year of perestroika, with its emphasis on decentralization and self-sufficiency, combined with growing problems of obtaining funds from the centralized sources, Mikhail decided to become an independent director of the choir. During the short period when he was responsible for 40 people, members of the choir as well as himself and his family, he acquired first-hand knowledge of operating in an environment of self-reliance and responsibility. The feeling was exciting and new. The new role was a challenge for Mikhail. He had to combine business and art and, as he said: 'getting the best results from both'.

Perestroika, however, was failing more and more to deliver the promised wealth and prosperity. The previously unknown phenomenon of inflation started to arise, wiping out people's incomes and savings. Attendance at the choir's performance started to fall. Mikhail had to concentrate more on financial issues. In 1989 the limited state support stopped completely. In trying to preserve his ensemble, one of the solutions Mikhail saw was to open a satellite business, a trading company, to help him finance the choir. The idea was quite revolutionary at that time and proved unpopular with many of his colleagues.

At the beginning of the 1990s the system of centralized supply had broken down and state monopoly became a thing of the past. Trade became the most lucrative of activities. It did not require much investment and one could bail out easily. It also did not require any substantial knowledge. As Mikhail said, his motto was simple: 'buy cheap, sell dear'.

Of course there was a chance of being approached by racketeers, but through his relatives, and with the help of the local Cossack organization, he created a so-called 'roof' – a protection group which helped him to escort goods from town to town. Mikhail was happy paying for this kind of service (approximately 20 per cent of the profit), a fraction compared to the 40–60 per cent charged by some groups.

For several months Mikhail, using his knowledge of the regions of Russia and the connections he had gained during his concert activities, was earning enough money to pay the salaries of his musicians and rent. The variety of goods he was trading in was enormous, from St Petersburg crystal to children's clothes from the Ukraine. In spite of his efforts some of his colleagues began taking his work for granted. Some complained that they could lose their musical skills as a consequence of long periods of non-performing. Mikhail believes that the mentality of dependency formed during the communist years was to blame for these attitudes.

At the end of 1991 Mikhail had to stop his musical career completely. After paying his musicians for the last time he left them, moving fully into a one-man trading business.

Now looking back, he admits that the first commercial activity was extremely primitive. Initially he was selling out of the boot of his car. But gradually the business improved and subsequently Mikhail employed his father and later his brother. The number of his employees grew to four or five people, who were all relatives except for the accountant.

His breakthrough into 'big business' he associates with the inflation of 1992–3. At the end of 1992, through a close friend at the local branch of a state bank, he managed to obtain a large credit equivalent to $100,000 at an interest rate of 5 per cent a year. In 1992 annual inflation soared to 2500 per cent, the highest increase during the years of transformation. Mikhail used the loan to rent premises in the centre of Volgograd. The lease was very favourable because once again Mikhail used his contacts in the local administration. One of the senior administrators had been an admirer of Mikhail's Cossack Choir. Indeed the most lucrative deals were made with the help of people who knew, or had heard about, the choir. Many were in one way or another related to the Volga–Don Cossack culture.

Mikhail realized that the market was becoming more mature and saturated. Constant shortages were becoming increasingly a thing of the past, and specialization seemed to be the way forward. Again using his acquired business sense, Mikhail decided to concentrate on foodstuffs. Inflation wiped out people's savings, pushing, according to the official statistics, almost 70 per cent of the population below the poverty line. People were cutting their expenses to the minimum but good food products were the only essential requirement.

In 1992, while on business in St Petersburg, Mikhail met a Finnish businessman, working for a famous Finnish company. To start business with a well-established Western company was extremely appealing. It took Mikhail a year to persuade the Finns to take him seriously and to start doing business through him in Volgograd. Due to a history of close cooperation with the former Soviet Union, and to geographical proximity, the Finns knew the Russian realities better than most other Western businessmen, although even for them the Russian province was unknown territory. In order to demonstrate his commitment, Mikhail entered into a 50/50 partnership and become a sole distributor of the Finnish company's products in the region.

Finnish ice cream, with its superb quality and, what was probably more important at that time, packaging, was an immediate success in the provincial Russian city. The price of US$1 a piece, when average monthly salaries were less than US$100, was not low; nevertheless most people could afford one ice cream a month. A market of 5 million people in Volgograd and the surrounding area was enough to sustain a 100 per cent profit margin.

The desire to grow made Mikhail different from the thousands of entrepreneurs who started their businesses with one ultimate goal – to buy a big Western car. However, growth required investment. His attempts to obtain support from his Finnish partners were unsuccessful, and he approached a bank. There were no longer state banks and there was almost no credit available for small businesses.

Mikhail investigated small business support programmes and was informed by the city council that theoretically there were funds available, but it would take several months to obtain the necessary information and to complete an application. It was, however, more likely that any state money available would be given to Moscow-based small businesses with the 'right connections' and not to a small provincial businessman.

Using an old contact, who was now working as a bank manager in the newly established Volgograd Agro Bank, Mikhail secured a loan for 5 years at rates set at the bank's discretion. The rate was a bearable 25 per cent in 1993. Weekly gifts to the bank manager in the form of discretely wrapped large packages of Finnish ice cream and other dairy products sold at his store, were part of the conventional arrangement.

The money, and good relations with the city administration allowed Mikhail to open several ice cream cafés around the city and buy in Finland two big Volvo refrigerator lorries. The business was developing steadily. However, the Russian ice cream industry, famous and regarded with affection in the past, which had shrunk virtually into non-existence at the beginning of the 1990s, began producing again with much-improved quality and new attractive packaging. The local ice cream factory was constantly lobbying the city administration to prevent Mikhail's growth and development.

The struggle for his business shaped Mikhail's character and taught him how to present and sell his ideas, how to persuade important people. His persistence in obtaining what he thought was right, was becoming known among his associates as a Cossack frontier mentality.

Mikhail was starting to develop schemes for Volgograd: these included distribution, transport and retail – a fully integrated chain from entry of the product in Russia to sale in his own shops. He did not want to depend on anybody: this in itself could be dangerous. Using the bank's loan Mikhail purchased transportation, storage and freezers from Finland. By now he had three 40-ton Volvo freezer lorries. At that time there was some flexibility in customs duties and he managed to obtain the lorries virtually tariff-free because he had a 2-year lease–purchase agreement. In this case the state regulations became useful.

In the period up to 1994 Mikhail maximized his sales volumes. The new scheme involved the local Volgograd Agro bank in his business and the bank actually become an investor, paying off the loan. The future looked positive and business was developing steadily.

There were problems of course. One of them was the general instability of the Russian economy with its dollar inflation which was very often damaging to his import relations with the Finns. The rates had to be adjusted on a daily basis and the retail prices had to be changed accordingly. Often staff had to come to work an hour earlier to make new price tags.

Another problem was the constant danger of racketeers. Mikhail does not like to talk about it. The fact that he was popular among a vast number of people, some of whom enjoyed high positions in the city administration, the police and the federal security service (former KGB), and who knew him as an excellent singer of Cossack ballads and an owner of a very popular store and cafés, was a sufficient deterrent to racketeers. Of course he had to have security, but that was nothing compared to what was going on around him.

Most businesses had to pay. The small entrepreneurs (no matter how paradoxical it sounds) were glad to pay racket money to a criminal group as long as it was a criminal group with a modest appetite of 10–20 per cent of the profit. The worst that could happen was that an entrepreneur would be approached by different groups and the decision whom to pay and whom to ignore could easily cost the life of the businessman or the life of his family. When Mikhail was in Great Britain he could not believe that the high street shops have no arrangements with local racketeers. He still does not.

However, some unsuccessful bank operations, the lavish lifestyles of the bank's management (which included 2-week vacations in Bermuda for the senior management) and the building of a $30 million headquarters in the centre of Volgograd, put Agro Bank on the brink of collapse. In order to save its rapidly deteriorating position, the bank started to charge its clients (Mikhail included) extremely high interest rates. It was a downward spiral in which the bank was using all possible means to stabilize its position. Interest rates were almost 100 per cent per annum in 1994, and rose to 220 per cent in 1995, although inflation had stabilized by this time at 120 per cent in 1994 and 63 per cent in 1995.

At the same time Mikhail had started to invest in the construction of storage facilities. 'It was my biggest mistake', he admits. 'I should have known that in times like that one just can't plan for the future by tying up capital. But nobody taught me finance.' Mikhail had invested the major part of the loan in construction, using the profits from several cafés and the shop to pay off the increasing interest rates. In 1995 Mikhail estimated his business to be worth 10 billion roubles. The business which he started from scratch had grown substantially. At the end of the same year Mikhail had 150 employees.

However, the failing bank was pushing him to take on more loans, and promised to compensate him in the future for the high interest rates and losses. The friendship with the bank manager prevented Mikhail from assessing the situation critically. 'I was brought up believing people. If you drink with someone, if your families spend time together, you tend to believe that no matter what figures tell you, the friend will not let you down.'

However, the bank increased interest rates on an almost daily basis, at the same time ignoring its pledges to Mikhail. 'My life became work, work, work. I could not sleep. My family life started to crack.' Interest rates continued to rise. Michael tried to repay his credits, but his capital was tied up in construction.

Eventually at the end of 1995 the bank's assets were frozen by the central authority. The bank, a major investor in Mikhail's business, took him to court in order to reclaim all the credit given to him at once. In spite of the fact that the credit arrangements were for a 5-year period, the court decided in favour of the bank and Mikhail's property (cafés, vehicles and the property under construction) had to be sold. As a result 130 employees became redundant. 'That was probably the worst period of my life. I do not how I managed not to do something stupid like leave my family or worse. Many years of my work went down the drain.' The bank became bankrupt nevertheless, and its director is still under investigation and detained in Volgograd's prison. A total of US$5 million has disappeared without trace. In all this Mikhail managed to save one shop (his present one) and a small team of people. In the summer of 1996 he formed an independent company called 'Aelita', starting virtually from scratch again. However, former contacts helped. The Moscow subsidiary of the Finnish company helped as well, in spite of the fact that the Finns were also badly affected by the collapse of the same bank.

Now Mikhail employs 30 people in his one shop in the centre of Volgograd. Most of his supplies come from the Moscow subsidiary of the Finnish company. However, he also has approximately 50 suppliers of food products from the Volgograd region and other parts of Russia. The shop is open every day from 8 a.m. till 8 p.m., with a lunch break 2–3 p.m. Working hours are regulated by legislation. Staff work 77 hours per week for alternate weeks. This is the typical pattern for employment in the Russian retail industry. Mikhail does not have problems in employing good committed people. He enjoys a reputation for being fair. The average monthly salary in his shop is 1 million roubles (in October 1997), compared to the average of 600,000 that is typical in the region.

Mikhail believes that he has learned a lot. According to him he has become more cynical. He does not believe people as he used to. But he is committed to going on in this business. His dream is to find an honest and reliable Western partner and open a chain of fast-food stores. There he believes there is a future for him.

CASE STUDY TWO: ANATOLY

Anatoly is a linguist by profession and in his mid-50s. Single, energetic and enthusiastic by nature, he was among the first who wholeheartedly supported the ideas of the market economy, believing that he would be able to realize his intellectual and entrepreneurial potential.

Before 1991 Anatoly was a lecturer of German language at the Volgograd Pedagogical University. He liked his job, but was not happy with the salary. Once he tried to get a PhD but due to family problems he could not finish it. To be a university lecturer without a PhD meant earning approximately 140 roubles a month, slightly more than the receptionist at the same university. Anatoly believes that he has entrepreneurial abilities. Even during the Soviet period he often had ideas about how money could be earned, but fear of facing hostility to entrepreneurs, and fear of the legal system, prevented him from realizing them.

At the start of Gorbachev's experiment with cooperatives Anatoly left the university and decided to fulfil his long-time dream and ambition – to start his first honey business. The idea was to start production of good-quality honey using the very favourable conditions of the Volgograd countryside.

He does not like to remember this experience. After 3 years of working very hard, often living in the country for months, reading vast amounts of specialized literature, he gave up. It turned out that the idea of producing good-quality natural honey had come to many people living in Volgograd and the region, who had much more agricultural experience than he did. Competition very often turned into open warfare when beehives were burned down or stolen. There were also problems in selling the honey. The region was oversupplied. Anatoly tried to sell his honey at the Moscow market, but the transport costs were staggering, boosted by the necessary professional 'escorts' on the 600-mile journey to Moscow. The Moscow market Mafia also made him pay, which wiped out his profits completely.

The memory of this unhappy experience held Anatoly back from starting anything new for some time. Anatoly was doing *ad-hoc* translating and interpreting, but the business was very irregular. There were not many tourists coming to Volgograd, except during the three months of summer, and at the same time plenty of professional linguists were graduating year after year from the Pedagogical University.

In 1995 Anatoly decided to try again. The impulse was given by the announcement of a government programme selling, for a symbolic amount, land in the country, with the aim of attracting people into farming. Anatoly purchased approximately one-third of an acre for the price of 300,000 roubles or about US$60, with the idea of starting livestock farming. On this occasion Anatoly did some homework and found out that the price of milk is three times higher in the city than in the country, and the price of beef is twice as high. Anatoly was also attracted by the talk at governmental level about the necessity of supporting programmes for farmers.

Anatoly knew, as most Russians did, much about the state of Russian agriculture, and he thought that with his commitment and hard work, together with the help he would get from the state, he could make a difference at least on his farm. As in the honey business, Anatoly did not have any previous experience with livestock. The idea seemed simple enough: animals multiply, cows give milk. He had studied advanced biology at school. Anatoly was planning to hire a reliable worker who would live at the farm and who would take care of everyday problems there, while Anatoly would be in charge of the distribution of milk and meat in the city.

From a bankrupt collective farm Anatoly purchased three cows and 15 sows. He built a wooden shed for the cows and another for the pigs. He also had to build a place where he could spend the night and where a hired worker could live. The construction, no matter how basic, took most of the savings left after the purchase of the livestock. At the same time Anatoly applied to the local authorities for a grant.

The problems started from the very beginning. To find a good reliable worker turned out to be very difficult. No matter that many collective farms had closed and there were numerous unemployed people, not many of them expressed interest in being involved in Anatoly's project. Anatoly reflected: 'More than 70 years of Socialism had rooted out a sense of pride for the work people do. Country people had completely forgotten what it is to be responsible, make decisions for themselves. For so many years they were told what to do: when to harvest and when to sow. Now they do not want anything but to drink themselves unconscious. They are not attracted even by the high salaries, to say nothing of the potential benefits in the future.'

During the first year Anatoly had to change four workers. They were all lazy and did not care. As soon as Anatoly had gone back to the city, they started drinking. Animals were not fed, sometimes for days. In fact during our last interview Anatoly was desperately looking for a new candidate to replace his existing worker. Another constant problem was forage; to obtain it on a regular basis was very difficult. Anatoly does not have his own transport, which means that every time he has to ask the locals to help him out. Most of the village people treat him badly: 'They do not want to help even when I offer good payment. They treat me as an intruder, an alien. I do not drink, at least not as much as they do, and that does not help either. There are a few who are sympathetic to my efforts. They sometimes help, especially when they see that animals are not fed. Once someone called me anonymously to inform me that my worker was having *delirium tremens* and that my animals had not been fed for 3 days.'

The state support programmes for farmers never materialized. Anatoly prepared numerous documents, but eventually he gave up. The bureaucracy was taking too much of his time. Anatoly commented: 'I did not see the state at all until I started to sell my first pork.' Anatoly had firstly to invite a local medical official to inspect the meat from the first slaughtered animal. After a positive conclusion (visual inspection of the quality of the meat), Anatoly had to take the carcass to another medical officer who stamped it on behalf of the district veterinary authority. The third step included a trip to the sanitary station where he had to leave a large piece of meat for the final medical check. The people involved in the chain, knowing their own power, very often expect favours. They can speed up or slow down the process. There is also a small official payment involved at each stage.

After obtaining three certificates (spravky), Anatoly was allowed to sell the meat at the market. In order to do so he had to pay for a stall (the place is important, so it is not unusual to give some 'favours' to the person in charge of the marketplace). The place itself costs 30,000–40,000 roubles a day. Then of course one has to hire a professional cutter (that is another 50,000 roubles). The next step is to find someone to sell the meat for you, and that is another 50,000 roubles a day. At the end of each day there is another unavoidable payment to the local Mafia, who casually walk from stall to stall and collect the money. This payment is another 50,000 roubles.

Of course the easiest way would be to bring the meat to the state shop and sell it to them. But in this case the price of 1 kilogram of meat would be just 11,000 roubles, instead of the 15,000 Anatoly could get by selling it privately.

Milk is another problem. There is an oversupply of milk in Volgograd and Anatoly has neither storage facilities nor transport to take it to another region, say Rostov, where people say the price of milk is 50 per cent higher.

Anatoly knows that this enterprise is another failure. In fact he knew it a long time ago, after the first few months. At the moment he has 20 sows and 100 2–3-month-old piglets and 18 cows. He feels responsible for the animals. In fact he even gave names to his cows: 'I got emotionally attached to them. They all have different characters and personalities. I know it is probably wrong to take them so close to heart but I just could not help it. I would never have started all this, if I had known how difficult it would be.' Anatoly also knows that it would be very difficult to sell his business. At the moment he has decided to carry on. To survive the winter he needs to repair the pig-shed and make the cow-shed warmer. He hopes that the nearby collective farm will keep its promise and sell him cheap feed.

Through an old friend Anatoly knows that there will be a big group of German businessmen coming to Volgograd soon, and he hopes to get some interpreting work from them. The money would be helpful to buy vitamins which the piglets desperately need.

CASE STUDY THREE: VLADIMIR

An energetic, Western-looking businessman in his early 50s, Vladimir moved into private entrepreneurial activity relatively recently in 1994. Prior to that he held a chair at the local university, teaching and conducting research projects on hydraulic systems. In his academic career Vladimir was very successful by any standards. He had gained his PhD in engineering when he was 25, his 'big' doctorate when he was 38 and a full professorship at the age of 40. For Vladimir, 'University was my life. It was giving me an interesting job, good money, prestige and the respect of my peers. The nature of my research was, of course, non-political, so I did not feel an ideological pressure as did some of my colleagues, who taught, for example, economics or other people-related subjects.'

When Gorbachev's reforms started, and later Yeltsin's, he was very sceptical, believing that Russians, brought up under the communist system, could not be turned into capitalists. Comparing society with a complicated engineering system Vladimir is convinced that 'changes of this scale have to be evolutionary, which means not just gradual. They have to happen for at least a hundred years. All Russian history tells us that the Russians are not individualistic by nature, they tend to incline to community, collective actions, they have to be led by some authoritative figure. Give Russians freedom, remove the feared authority and one can get chaos and nothing else. Communism in its inhuman nature was evil, but it was good because it provided a strong authority without which Russians cannot exist and function.'

According to Vladimir the philosophy of individualism, the quality which is needed in the market economy, is a very rare quality among the Russian people. This belief, combined with the enjoyment which Vladimir was getting from his work, prevented him from thinking about self-employment until the summer of 1994. Vladimir remembers that: '1992 and 1993 were extremely difficult years for me and my family. Inflation was going wild, reaching more then 2000 per cent at the end of 1992. It seemed at that time that the whole world was just collapsing around us. Students were leaving the university in droves, unable to cope with the increasing cost of living, attracted by the opportunities of getting big money just by straightforward commercial activity. [The drop-out rate soared from 2–3 per cent in 1990 to 22 per cent in 1993.] My university colleagues, realizing much more quickly than myself that prestige and money at the university were things of the past, were leaving their jobs, moving into trade, often travelling to Moscow, where they could buy consumer goods more cheaply and then sell them at a higher price in Volgograd. One does not have to have a PhD for this type of activity. To watch all of this was very sad.' In 1993 Vladimir's salary in real terms went down by 60 per cent compared to the pre-reform years. On average an unqualified manual worker was paid more than a university professor.

Through the nature of Vladimir's academic research he happened to know very many of the managers of the major industrial enterprises in the city. The old system of academic research encouraged cooperation between academics and industry. There were many projects which Vladimir had conducted for and with large enterprises in Volgograd and Moscow. Continuing to have good relations, often at the personal level, with them, Vladimir knew about their current problems, brought about by liberalization of prices, inflation, decreased amount of financial support from the centre and catastrophic lack of liquidity.

The last factor was the most worrying. Employees were not being paid for months at a time, and barter between enterprises, and enterprises and workers, when wages were paid in kind, seemed to be the dominant form of economic relations. To break the circle of barter and find access to real money was one of the main objectives of the majority of enterprises in Volgograd.

Vladimir's analytical skills, developed during his academic career, personal acquaintance with the directors and managers of very many of the industrial enterprises in Volgograd and in Moscow, combined with the rapidly deteriorating standard of living of himself and his family, were the main factors which influenced his decision to leave the university and start his own one-man business. The last, but not the least, factor for him was that he 'refused to be humiliated by the miserable salaries paid at the university, and the loss of respect for the intellectual type of activity which does not bring immediate monetary benefits'.

Vladimir's idea of what his business would be, was very simple: to find a cash payer and match buyers and sellers. Vladimir's first business transaction required 'one day of hard thinking and drawing up schemes, approximately one hundred telephone calls and several hours of hard negotiations'. In the period of a couple of weeks, through his numerous contacts, Vladimir collected information about the real needs of the 16 largest enterprises in Volgograd. He prepared sophisticated barter schemes for each of them, found traders in Moscow and the region willing to buy some of the goods at a discount, and negotiated for himself a fee, often also in kind, from each of the parties involved. Vladimir admits that only his personal acquaintance with the managers and directors opened the door for him and made the business successful.

This first commercial activity brought Vladimir a remuneration unheard of when he was at the university. In just 2 weeks he had earned six times as much as his annual salary as a professor.

Vladimir has now been in business for 3 years. He has become tougher, and has developed his negotiation and bargaining skills. There are 1500 business telephone numbers in his personal electronic diary.

Vladimir misses his academic life badly. From time to time, when nostalgia becomes hard to cope with, he goes to the university where he is always welcome. However, after these visits, seeing the poor state of the university and the miserable salaries of his colleagues, he feels better, believing that the decision to give up his academic career was the correct one.

Money is not a problem any more. He drives a new expensive SAAB and wears Armani suits. His wife does not work and his only son attends the most exclusive private business college. Vladimir is thinking of sending him to Britain to study for his degree. In the summer Vladimir plans to buy two adjacent three-bedroom apartments, connect them and establish a flat and his office in one place. He would like to buy a house but he is concerned about security issues.

Vladimir's business is becoming more competitive. There are more companies sorting out barter on the market and if, in the past, the directors were responding to his offers with enormous gratitude, now he has often to bribe them, in order to secure exclusive rights to represent them. Still he believes that there is plenty of work for him in the years to come: 'My business is a peculiar one. In fact there are thousands like mine. Whether I like it or not, the worse the situation is in the country, the better it is for me. As soon as there is a stabilized federal budget and a proper market economy with working institutions, there will not be much work left for me. However, I do not believe that I should worry too much about it. For the years to come the economy will be in need of businesses like mine.'

Vladimir's analytical logic suggests that it is dangerous to rely on one business only, no matter how good it is. So currently he has two further potentially very profitable ventures. One of them is a joint television venture, of which he owns 95 per cent and a private American company the other 5 per cent. Another business is an ecological research centre in which he is the director. The centre is supposed to be financed by the federal budget, although there is not much money coming in at the moment. Vladimir believes that ecological problems are so severe in the city that sooner or later the authorities will understand the importance of this research and will provide the funding for it.

In spite of his personal success Vladimir is very pessimistic about the future of reforms and of Russian small business in particular. His scepticism is based on the belief of the communal nature of Russians, their inability to be motivated solely by money over the long term and a general lack of entrepreneuralism in people. When confronted with his experience, Vladimir is convinced that he is not typical and he would willingly abandon his economic activities as soon as the university offered decent conditions again.

CONCLUDING REMARKS

The development of small business does not happen in a vacuum. Its successes and failures largely depend on the continuity of institutional change in Russia and its regions, particularly in the legislative, financial and behavioural areas. The speed at which small businesses have appeared shows that millions of people have an enormous creative potential, which had been suppressed during the communist regime for over 70 years.

The experience of the Western countries confirms that small businesses can make a substantial, if not critical, contribution to economic development, institutional change and economic growth. This is even more true for transitional economies. Small businesses can contribute greatly to the stabilization of Russia by absorbing a large part of the labour force made redundant by restructuring. Small business can act as educational institutions, providing first-hand knowledge of the basics of a market economy. It can also provide much-needed goods and services for consumers and also for large-scale enterprises, and can help to create a competitive environment, increasing the allocative and productive efficiency of the market.

On the other hand, left on their own, small businesses are often confronted by a corrupt and inefficient bureaucracy, lack of funds and 'expert competence necessary to set-up enterprises,... necessary skills needed for sales, marketing and financial management' (Scase, 1997:19). Small businesses are targeted by criminals, virtually ignored by commercial banks and often they cannot even acquire proper insurance cover. They are surrounded by an inefficient and unsupportive tax system. Such a negative experience, gained while working in the small business sector, could be a fertile ground for breeding disillusionment with transition on a mass scale. The absence of a coherent, comprehensive and realistic government programme, aimed at helping small businesses, could discredit the whole idea of entrepreneurship.

The current situation affecting farmers illustrates this point. For many years the Russian government has stressed the importance of private farming in Russia. However, there has been virtually no support from the government and the state budget. The funds, allocated to agriculture, were first divided between dying, inefficient collective farms, and what was left (often nothing) was given to private farmers (*Moskovskie Novosti*, no. 52, 1998:3). Not surprisingly, during the seven years since 1991, the share contributed by private farmers to the total production of agricultural goods was no higher than 1–2 per cent. Now farmers are accused of being unproductive. The conclusion which is drawn by opponents of entrepreneurship is that 'if they [private farmers] disappear altogether, the economy will not suffer' (*ibid.*). The consequences of this kind of logic could be devastating for the Russian transformation.

Part III
Analysis and Prognosis

8 Managers' Views

INTRODUCTION

As part of our investigation of companies' responses and adaptation to change, a questionnaire survey was conducted amongst managers of two of Volgograd's well-established enterprises: the Tractor Plant and the Parts Plant. Managers at the plants were asked to answer a range of questions relating to the changes which the respective enterprises had undergone over the previous 5 years.

The questionnaire responses were subsequently collated and analysed using content analysis (Holsti, 1969) and Mendelow's power/interest matrix (Johnson and Scholes, 1997:198). This matrix allowed the authors to focus on the role and significance of individual stakeholders in the respective enterprises and to chart changes in relative stakeholder interest and power. Stakeholders can display varying levels of interest in a particular organization. However, it is normally the degree of power exercised by stakeholders which can have the greatest influence and impact.

STRUCTURE OF THE ENTERPRISE

Substantial changes had taken place. The traditional structures had been smashed, with a new importance being attached to accounting, finance and distribution as well as to suppliers and the quality of inputs. The role and activity of planning, production and R&D had declined. The enterprises now had a simpler structure: some departments had been merged. New positions had also been established. For example, at the Tractor Plant there was now a commercial director who had responsibility for distribution and retailing and was in charge of the Technical Trade Centre. There was also a new internal security structure; a further innovation was the appointment of a departmental director for external relations. The significance of the quality control department had also increased.

The structure of the enterprise was now more transparent. However, there was felt to be a need for greater flows of information between departments at the same level of the organization; that is,

137

there was a noticeable need to pass information horizontally rather than vertically.

These changes had been contemporaneous with a large decline in the volume of production and redundancies among administrative staff. Managers felt that they were being utilized more effectively and the overall quality of management had risen.

New organization structures included departments for accounting and finance and for advertising. The Tractor Plant had also developed its external relations. For example, each shop (production unit) now had its own marketing function. The enterprise had also set up its own trading house as well as subsidiaries in other Russian regions and in the members of the CIS.

At the same time informal structures had been weakened. The role and influence of the trades unions had declined significantly. The enterprise no longer provided its employees with social services such as housing. The unions had been a key instrument of the enterprise, for instance, in organizing socialist competition. This was now disbanded. Now the trades union could not even guarantee the payment of employees' wages.

The key goal of enterprise strategy was survival. Managers felt that employees understood the recovery plan. Levels of employment were currently stable. A major element of the enterprise's strategy was to raise quality, which would require a change in commercial and technical policies. The enterprise needed to increase sales volume and the cash conversion ratio. The enterprise needed to be profitable irrespective of the price charged for its products. It had to dispose of enormous stocks of products, and needed to produce what was actually in demand. One of the enterprise's aims was to raise the volume of orders from customers in the West. However, at the moment there were insufficient customers who were in a position to pay. Sales were perceived as the key to the successful achievement of the enterprise's strategy; related to this was a need to develop new products.

There was a general view that there was a need for continuous change. More effort needed to be put into: expanding the distribution and sales network; developing production and R&D; and improving the financial dimension. In spite of the structural changes, the organization structure was still regarded as inflexible and functioned only because of innumerable meetings. There was a need for greater informal interaction, both horizontally between departments and vertically. Some managers felt that there was a need for senior management to exert their influence informally rather than just through formal structures. As one of the managers noted: 'We still do not communicate well with each other. We are good at receiving orders and passing them further down, but we do not know how to talk about our common tasks to our colleagues in the parallel structures. Often the only way in which we do communicate is when we criticize the boss. As soon as we realize that the only way to overcome our common difficulties is to talk to each other in order to achieve joint solutions, things will improve.'

The implementation of the enterprise's strategy required discipline and self-discipline. One approach would be to introduce performance-related pay. A flexible structure needed to be developed in order to respond to the changes in the external environment.

The interviewees at the Parts Plant identified a number of changes in the structure of the enterprise, including the setting up of commercial and marketing departments, the technical trading centre, and the quality control department (reporting to the managing director). As the information structures of the previous system were dying out, new informal relationships were evolving. For example, there was a 'brain centre' consisting of the MD, chief technologist, chief engineer and the commercial and financial directors. The MD and his subordinates were now learning how to use these informal relationships. At another level the Parts Plant has become a joint-stock company, with the general assembly of stakeholders as its main body.

The company's strategy was seen as comprising a number of strands, with the general aim of making progress with economic and financial restructuring. There was a need to reduce indebtedness, obtain working capital (this is currently non-existent), improve the cost structure by reducing the input of raw materials, broaden the product range and raise quality (e.g. via ISO 9000 certification). It was strongly felt that the company needed to supply the market with what it really wanted. As the marketing director said: 'The marketing textbook rule that one has to produce not what he or she can but what the market needs, is gradually getting through to people. Not, however, as fast as we want.'

To achieve this the company needed to analyse the requirements of various markets and find appropriate market niches. The company was keen to achieve stability under market conditions. Furthermore, innovation in all aspects of the company's activities was essential: too many people were working, but were not being driven by the company's objectives.

The interviewees believed that the company's strategy was generally understood. However, the degree of horizontal coordination and understanding was poor. It was not clear what the responsibilities of each department were, and individuals were still reluctant to assume individual responsibility for their work. Many employees still clung to the notion of collective responsibility. Many managers believed that the centre needed to provide more information and feedback in this area.

The volume of production had fallen enormously because of the collapse of the internal market and the loss of the COMECON markets. Old ties needed to be renewed. A key factor was farmers' lack of money. Price liberalization had killed off business. The situation was characterized by lack of liquidity and mutual indebtedness. A major problem was seen to be the state, in particular taxation policy and the absence of state involvement in energy sector pricing. As one respondent explained: 'The state has to understand its responsibility for the situation in our economy and in our enterprise. Before [the reforms] the state was like a good and forgiving mother and not really a very demanding mother. Now the state acts as if the only thing it is interested in are taxes and taxes and nothing else. Its policy actually adds to our problems.'

The company needed to rejuvenate its product range by abandoning obsolete products and developing new ones. This would require an expansion of the R&D applied to products and production, and an increase in specialist staff. Such a policy would also depend on investment and consequently access to credits. The company also needed to improve its relationships with the agro-industrial complex.

PRODUCTION

All aspects of the transformation had been detrimental to production. The most crucial factor had been the loss of the markets of the former Soviet Union; another factor had been the disappearance of COMECON (including its non-European members). As a result of the loss of these markets the production of agricultural machinery was no longer so significant. The main problem, however, was the lack of cash to upgrade production.

Managers at the Tractor Plant admitted to the existence of military production within the enterprise, though they did not know or did not wish to disclose the extent of this military production. It appeared that this area of activity, although declining, offered more stability than tractors.

There was a broad consensus that a restructuring of production was very important. There was a need to introduce new technology but this needed to go hand in hand with the identification of markets. However, there were divergent views on what form restructuring should actually take. These views included on the one hand diversification into new products and services, on the other hand a desire to increase the enterprise's self-sufficiency in order to achieve greater stability and increase employment. A contrary view was to slim down the enterprise by hiving off activities such as steel production.

The managers were sceptical about the feasibility of attracting investment into the enterprise. While FDI was considered for some a remote possibility, it was felt that no substantial attempts had been made to attract it. Some managers were of the opinion that investors could not be guaranteed a proper use of their investment and there was no certainty that the enterprise would be turned into profitability. One commented: 'Of course we would like to have investment, we would love it. But we are not as naive as we were some years ago. The West does not want to help, it wants profits and security and we cannot guarantee either, not now anyway.'

There was a view that any FDI would be channelled into paying off debt and taxes rather than into investment. Federal legislation was considered crucial to create an environment conducive to FDI.

FINANCE

Mutual indebtedness has increased enormously since the market reforms. The Tractor Plant owed just under 70 billion roubles and was owed 72 billion roubles. The bulk of indebtedness was tied up in charges for energy. A number of proposals were made on how to clear inter-company indebtedness. These included: wiping the slate clean; restructuring debts over a 10-year period; the provision of interest-free credits to pay wages and salaries; finding a bank willing to accept the company's shares as a loan guarantee; finding cash purchasers for the company's products; and changing the tax base. Managers also felt that the enterprise needed to learn how to conduct barter effectively and operate with promissory notes.

The finance department was playing an increasing role in areas such as accounting and financial management. It was felt that the department had an 'independent' role and its influence would increase.

There was a certain nostalgia for the former State Ministry. The state no longer provided any support and is now regarded as a hindrance. Previously investment came from the state. Now it had to come out of profits which are insufficient or from bank credits (which are not redeemable). Purely internal accumulation (profits and depreciation) was small; consequently very little investment was taking place. The enterprise was carrying out some production for payment in cash but this activity was regarded as limited.

The Parts Plant needed massive investments to implement its strategy. It was estimated that between 16 and 20 billion roubles would be required to settle debts. Investment from sources external to the company was also mentioned: there was a need to identify potential Russian investors; foreign investment might become possible when the company's products achieved a certain degree of international recognition. The Ukraine was specifically mentioned with regard to improving trade relations.

With regard to indebtedness the company was owed far more than it itself owed. It was estimated that the balance in favour of the company exceeded 10 billion roubles. A number of strategies to improve liquidity had been identified and were being implemented, including: finding new markets; making management and production more efficient; analysing demand; finding cash buyers and becoming more involved in retailing.

The company's finance department was now acting completely differently from the past. It was needing to look for money, to pressurize debtors and find new ways of clearing mutual debts and credits. Previously, the department had been merely producing reports of the current situation. It had now become, as one interviewee described it, 'the heart of the enterprise' on which the company depended for its well-being. The interviewees were of the view that further investment in the development of the finance department was needed.

The company no longer receives any financial support from the state and here too the state was regarded as making life difficult. Previously, the state had provided the enterprise with investment funds; now these had to come out of the company's profits.

R&D

R&D at the Tractor Plant was previously funded by the Ministry; there was also a fund for the development of production. Since the reforms there has been central government support only for military conversion. There was a recognition that R&D was very important but it now had to be funded solely out of the company's profits.

Some managers were of the view that R&D was possible only if there were central government support – but this no longer existed. It seemed that only small-scale projects were being undertaken in house and that some other work was being undertaken by associated research institutes. One manager commented: 'It's a shame that so much of our research potential is not needed any more. We have well-qualified people full of ideas, but we have hardly any finances to make the R&D more systematic. The state does not help and we cannot even pay the wages of our workers, to say nothing of investing in research. But even the lowliest worker knows that without research there are no new products and there is not much of a future.'

A similar situation prevails at the Parts Plant. The company tries to carry out R&D but only at a very low level because of lack of funds. The implications of this situation are frightening as there is no future without R&D. Most R&D as well as equipment is outdated. There is no money to increase the level of R&D, though there has been a proposal to create a small, mobile group of 'eggheads' to raise standards of products and production.

MARKETING

The Tractor Plant had established a marketing department since the reforms. It was regarded as a vital coordinating mechanism, without which it would be impossible to survive. The department had established subsidiaries in a number of Russian regions and the CIS.

The members of the marketing department were young and technically well educated. However, they had no marketing knowledge or experience and the department did not employ any marketing professionals. As one of the managers said: 'Our marketing people are among the youngest at the Plant. I believe that because of their age they do not have a burden of knowledge of past distribution policies. They have a lot to learn and they soon will become marketing experts. That is what we desperately need.'

The competitive situation in tractors was complex. Before the reforms there had been four major tractor manufacturers (in the same range of tractors) in the Soviet Union. In addition to the Volgograd Tractor Company (TC) there had been the Altaisky TC,

Kharkovsky TC (now in the Ukraine) and Pavlodarsky TC (now in Kazakhstan). Volgograd TC was the sole remaining company in its class in Russia and, with the collapse of the agro-industrial complex, was utilizing only 15 per cent of its capacity. Although currently not competing significantly with Volgograd TC, Altaisky TC and Pavlodarsky TC represented potential future competition. The same circumstances applied to foreign competitors. Imports were in comparative terms very expensive and more difficult to use. There were some signs of foreign competition – this was currently minimal but it was feared that it would increase.

Before the reforms, exports accounted for 5–7 per cent of output. Export sales had collapsed and were at a very low level of $1-1\frac{1}{2}$ per cent of output. Most exported tractors had been destined for other COMECON countries, with a small number going to the developing countries and China. Previously, 40 per cent of output had gone to Belorussia, Ukraine, Kazakhstan and Moldova; now less than 1 per cent of output was shipped to other CIS states.

Distribution is now the responsibility of the marketing department. A major problem is that potential buyers do not have cash, and relationships with customers lack stability. The department promotes the company's products by means of advertising, exhibitions and representatives based in Russia and abroad.

The momentous upheavals which have taken place have affected but not destroyed completely the old ties that existed. The close relationships between the company and the agricultural sector have been diluted. Contacts with foreign partners formerly within the USSR have become more complex because of tariff barriers, different currencies and barter. The most significant aspect of current commercial activity is that around 85 per cent of sales involve barter.

The changes have provided only limited scope for developing the product range and between 80 and 90 per cent of products have remained unchanged. There is a new tractor (the VT100) and some diversification into earth-moving equipment.

The Parts Plant too did not have a marketing department previously, but new departments had now emerged and were increasingly operating as described in the Western literature. However, as at the Tractor Plant, the marketing department did not employ any marketing professionals. There was also a clear recognition that the company's knowledge of marketing was insufficient. Top managers would benefit from lectures on marketing. Some managers wanted the marketing department to teach other departments how to identify new markets. The company needed to add about 10 per cent new products each year to its product range in order to attract new customers.

Before the reforms there had been some competition from the Beloretsky plant. Competition had intensified, both locally and in the country as a whole, although many managers were unclear who the company's competitors actually were. One manager, however, was able to name nine significant competitors from across Russia.* There was now also some competition from abroad, e.g. imported spanners from Germany.

In the past the Parts Plant had overwhelmingly supplied the internal market, although the company had supplied some spare parts to COMECON countries which had purchased products manufactured in the USSR, such as tractors.

A substantial proportion of output (though estimates varied substantially) was directed to former states of the Soviet Union, in particular Belarus, Kazakhstan and Uzbekistan. The company was eager to increase sales to these countries and also to the Ukraine. The expansion of sales was being driven by the commercial and marketing departments and a new retailing outlet had been opened.

Indebtedness had resulted in a close relationship with certain companies, though these depended substantially on personal relationships of the MD. Good relationships had also been maintained with 10 of the company's traditional customers. One respondent explained that: 'Only personal trust allowed us to retain the old customers. In fact these relationships survived against, probably, all economic logic. All of us lived through a very hard time but we trusted in each other and helped each other to survive.' In these relationships barter played a very significant role; 80 per cent of sales involved barter. As one manager stated, 'Barter is the king.'

Many of the old ties had been broken but the company was now trying to renew them. Around 20–5 per cent of the old ties were still active. For example, in the past the company had 120 customers who supplied around 200 agricultural technical centres. The company had retained contact with only 30 of these original customers. Furthermore the range of products had declined and around a quarter of products had changed.

---

* These included companies in Belorets, Belebeger, Saratov, Magnetogorsk, Orlov and Moscow.

SOCIAL DIMENSION OF THE ENTERPRISE

Before the reforms the Tractor Plant had substantial social facilities including 6000 square metres of living space in around 30 dormitories, about 30 kindergartens, a stadium and palace of culture (for recreational activities).

The enterprise has already transferred nine dormitories to the city administration and is trying to relinquish responsibility for a similar number. The enterprise does not have the resources to maintain these facilities and plans to transfer all living accommodation and kindergartens to the municipality. The enterprise also used to have recreation sites on the River Don and pioneer camps. Its House of Young Technicians, which was aimed at schoolchildren and teenagers, is still being supported but this facility is also likely to be transferred or closed.

All in all, there is little left of the social infrastructure which existed before the reforms and what remains will most probably disappear. There have been enormous changes in the role played by living accommodation. Before the reforms workers with between 10 and 20 years' service received free accommodation. Now accommodation goes to those who can afford to pay for it and length of service no longer counts. It was normal to have to wait 10–12 years before being allocated a place in enterprise accommodation. Nowadays there is very limited construction taking place, which creates difficulties for the enterprise and its workers. As one manager reflected: 'The employees who were most upset were those who were at the top of the waiting list for accommodation, just before everything started falling down [i.e. the 'economic reforms' – authors]. Some of them left the enterprise but some still hope that the construction of the apartments will start again. Otherwise there is no way for people to get decent accommodation.'

Previously a substantial range of leisure activities were organized by the enterprise, including outings to the countryside and evenings in the palace of culture. Nowadays, providing and paying for entertainment have become too expensive. Furthermore, the trades unions are short of money. The trades unions have retained only the recreational facilities on the Volga River. There has been a substantial shift from leisure activities organized and supported by the enterprise and trades unions to individual forms of recreation such as fishing and hunting, spending time at the dacha, but also holidays abroad.

The changes have also affected sporting activities, which have suffered a drastic decline and are dying out. The enterprise's sports stadium has been rented out and now accommodates a public market. Moreover, the trades unions are in no position to hold back the commercialization of sporting facilities. As one manager commented: 'Survival is more important than sport.'

The enterprise's catering facilities have been similarly affected. Before the reforms the enterprise had 27 canteens with 430 employees. There are now only five canteens employing 110 staff and these are used to only 15–20 per cent of their capacity. The main difficulty is that the prices are too expensive for the workforce who cannot afford to pay up to US$1.50 for a meal.

The major difficulty with the social infrastructure is the lack of resources. Previously the finance for the social infrastructure came from the central ministry; now it has to come out of the company's profits or, as in the case of the kindergartens, from the children's parents. In all this, the trades union is powerless.

Social activities at the Parts Plant were now being 'driven' by one female employee. Previously the company had three kindergartens and a pioneer camp on the River Don. It now had only one kindergarten and a recreational facility on the other side of the Volga.

In the past the company had been engaged in substantial housing construction and employees had to join a waiting list for company accommodation. There was no longer any free accommodation and new housing construction had ceased, although the company was trying to complete existing projects.

Company-based recreational activities had virtually ceased. Previously the company had arranged holidays by the sea for which there had been special discount vouchers. Now there was neither money nor vouchers. Sporting activities were just surviving, largely because of individual enthusiasm. Employees could still attend a swimming pool twice a week free of charge.

Catering had been good in the past and had continued to be so, but was now considered expensive, although it was now beginning to recover from the shock of price increases. There was some optimism that the range of social activities would expand again once sales improved.

DISTRICT AND CITY AUTHORITIES

Before the reforms there had been a close relationship between the Tractor Plant and the local authorities which had exercised tight control over the company's activities. There had been a two-way flow of requests and support. Now the company was able to be more independent but conversely received less support. There was still mutual respect and loyalty but the relationship had become more business-like. The respective organizations understood each other's needs but lacked the resources to act as they had done in the past.

Relations between the company and the city authorities had taken a turn for the better since the arrival of the new management team and were now considered excellent because of the efforts of the MD. There were plans to increase the range of social activities when sales improved. One respondent expressed the changing relationship between the company and the city authorities in the following way: 'Before the reforms we [enterprise and local authorities] were like in a marriage without love: suspicious of each other, forced to care for each other in formal relations established by Party Committees. Now we are free and the relations which we have are our own. We are partners with local administrations, sharing the same objectives: keep people in employment, try paying them for what they have earned, get the plant right because healthy enterprises mean healthier local finances.'

LABOUR

The number of employees at the Tractor Plant had halved over the past 5 years, from 29,000 at the beginning of 1992 to 13,700 at the beginning of 1997. Because production had fallen considerably, there was great instability, wages had declined and were not always paid on time. Many employees had left voluntarily, seeking better opportunities elsewhere, or were dissatisfied with the job and wages, although other factors for leaving included ill-health and reaching pensionable age. However, most of the leavers were young workers with relatively low levels of qualification (e.g. secondary school leaving certificate) and no commitments. These leavers faced an uncertain future and many had expressed a desire to return to the enterprise. The departure of these younger workers resulted in an increase in the overall qualification level of the company, even though no new graduates were taken on.

Administrative employees also declined in numbers (from 6700 in 1992 to 4000 in 1997). The decline was less than the overall average because of the establishment of new departments for marketing, training, etc.

The nature of work has also become more demanding, with hence an increased requirement for qualified labour. The level of discipline has increased, although sometimes there is no work to be done because of the lack of orders. There is virtually no labour turnover now, though absenteeism has risen since 1992.

Previously, workers were attracted to the enterprise by the social benefits it offered, in particular accommodation and the general social infrastructure, although the company's reputation and wages were also considered important. Nowadays, being employed and receiving a wage were in themselves sufficient, as jobs were very difficult to obtain.

In the past the workers' main concerns were wage levels, accommodation and the nature of work. Nowadays workers are mainly concerned by not having a job, getting paid on time, the survival of the company, wage levels and working conditions. Many managers believe that the workers do not understand the changes and do not believe in them: 'Workers do not believe in changes any more, nor do they understand them well. Very many of them are disillusioned and bitter. Their life became very difficult after the reforms. Privatization was supposed to change all that, but it did not. Many of them just tired of politics and hearing about yet another corruption scandal at the government level.' One manager, however, commented that the workers did understand the changes but that many senior managers did not believe in them.

The influence of the trades unions had declined, in some managers' view, dramatically. In the past the trades unions had represented stability and a certain kind of charity. Many people still seemed to believe in them in spite of their powerlessness. The trades unions were no longer involved in decision making, neither in the productive nor the social sphere. An isolated view was that because of its independence the trades union was not afraid of anything.

In spite of the changes it was felt that attitudes within the enterprise had remained positive and there was a climate of cooperation between the workers and other groups of employees. Employees were also acting more responsibly than in the past – this was attributed to the competition for jobs in the labour market. Employees were motivated by a need to earn their wages and by being paid on time (even though managers felt that a delay of up to 3–4 months was acceptable to the workforce).

The workforce displayed both fear and passivity. Many workers are afraid that they will lose their jobs. Overall many workers continue to work honestly (rather than 'helping themselves'). There are, however, numerous incidences of pilfering and theft.

'Theft has increased because workers are not always paid and things are easy to sell. In the past workers pilfered largely for themselves. Now at the open market one can sell and buy everything. People steal more because they can sell it more easily and in bigger quantities.'

The general climate was not helped by the general instability of the government and by the decline of the social infrastructure.

Labour productivity has declined considerably (between five- and ten-fold) during the period of market reforms. This decline has been caused mainly by external factors. Consequently the production cycle has become very erratic. Managers felt it very important to secure a normal pace of production. The continuing existence of inefficient enterprises was considered a drain on resources which could be used to better effect in enterprises such as the Tractor Plant. Some managers felt that there ought to be a new starting point including a new, more motivating taxation policy.

At the Parts Plant the number of employees had declined from around 3600 in 1991 to 2000 in 1997. Many of the employees who had left had been young and able to find employment elsewhere. As a consequence the average age of the workforce had risen from 40 to 42. The changed circumstances placed far tougher demands on the workforce.

The number of administrative employees had been affected largely by two factors: the substantial decline in output and employment (this had a negative impact on the need for administrative staff); and the need to internalize functions which had previously been carried out by the ministry (this increased the need for administrative staff). The number of administrative staff had as a consequence increased proportionately, if not absolutely. There was also some indication of a shift from collective to individual responsibility.

Demands on the workforce have risen because of the more competitive market conditions, the fear of unemployment and the arrival of the new MD. The outcomes of centralized planning had been very chaotic; now the workforce was subject to a more systematic approach to the organization of production. The morale of the workforce had in general declined because of the non-payment of wages and the irregularity of work. Conversely, discipline had been increased (some said because of the new MD).

In the past people had wanted to work for the company because it paid above-average wages, because of the geographical location of the plant, its social infrastructure, the possibility of free accommodation and the stability of the labour collective. In spite of the current difficulties, the company was still regarded as paying above-average wages regularly. It also paid employees' medical insurance. However, the main motivation for working for the company now was that, compared to other companies, it continued to provide regular wages.

Previously employees had no worries. Now they were concerned about the general situation of instability, job insecurity and the irregularity of wage payments. A key issue was getting the workforce to understand and believe in the new ways of working. A lot of effort was going into explaining the situation. Often words and deeds failed to coincide. Even if individual workers demonstrated greater personal responsibility, it was felt that there was still much improvement to be made in this area.

Employees were 'motivated' by the fear of losing their jobs, although in the view of some managers this was not as important as the attractiveness of the job itself, the stable moral–psychological climate prevailing in the company and self-respect and professional pride. Employees were often passive because of the lack of regular work and payment.

Pilfering at the Parts Plant had continued, but the opportunities to do so had diminished since the discovery of large-scale theft from the stores.

OWNERSHIP CHANGES

Changes in the ownership of the enterprises had also caused other changes. Employment had become more stable. However, it was felt that the workers had not been affected by this and retained a mentality of dependency. The change of ownership had so far done little to change work attitudes. Shareholders did not feel any benefits to ownership as the company had not yet declared any dividends. The workforce was considered to understand that strikes were a useless instrument, and in general a satisfactory work atmosphere prevailed.

Social support for the workforce had also changed, but they were still guaranteed wages (in spite of the irregularity of payment) and workers with families still enjoyed preferential treatment; for example they had better working conditions.

MANAGEMENT

The demands on managers had changed completely from the past. In the past they merely carried out orders. Now they had to be proactive and knowledgeable (for example with regard to Western management theories). Today professionalism (rather than party affiliation) was considered essential. One manager described key managerial characteristics in the following way: mobility, romanticism, devotion, energy and a calculating mind.

As with other issues, funding for training and retraining was limited to what the company could afford out of its profits. In the past the ministries and other bodies had provided funds for training, or actual training. Managers had gone to Moscow and Rostov and even abroad for training courses. However, many of these courses had been very formal and had been detached from the real problems of the enterprise. The inability to attend courses of the kind that had been offered in the past was not considered a great loss. However, the need to be appropriately qualified was considered important (according to one manager 'as important as air'). Some top managers were trying to raise their own level of expertise by, for example, attending courses at a regional quality centre. French and German quality agencies were running seminars on quality for senior managers. The company, however, did not offer any courses and, because of financial constraints, such external courses were at present out of the question. Western trainers did not seem to have made any noticeable inroads in Volgograd.

There was general agreement that managers now exercised greater power than in the past and the number of 'management' issues had risen. There were also many examples of managers, including senior managers at director level, leaving the company to join or set up private companies. Conversely there were virtually no cases of new managers joining the company.

There appeared on the whole to be a considerable stability of the management group. The vast majority of senior and middle managers had remained with the company. Those who had left the company had tended to be either technical specialists or workers who were dissatisfied with the level of wages and the irregularity of payment. Only a few employees had chosen to go into retirement.

There was a feeling that many managers were ambivalent to the changes being experienced by the country and the company. They understood the need for change but rejected the methods by which it was being implemented. They expressed no interest in the general problems of the transformation but were concerned by the crisis in their branch of industry; for example, by the company's underutilized capacities. As might be expected, there was a broad spectrum of views, from rejection of the transformation to a realistic evaluation of the current situation. Some managers were, however, frustrated because some people expressed the view that the company did not need managers.

Managers felt that above all they needed stability. There were too many debates about wage differentials and the withdrawal of state subsidies. Managers need to become more qualified and experienced, to update their knowledge continuously in spite of lack of time to do this. Most managers had received no training for the previous 5 years. Managers also need to assume more responsibility for, and take greater care of, younger managers in order to help them to develop.

Managers generally believed they had more (some said much more) power. Managerial power had not been given but taken, and power led to profit. One interviewee commented that although managers lack education and understanding of the situation, they worry most about their own salaries, which were very high, in spite of the decline in production. As one manager exclaimed: 'They've got everything!'

CONCLUSION

A number of formerly significant external stakeholders, that is the Ministry and the Communist Party, had disappeared as significant forces within the enterprises. Of other stakeholders the power of the trades unions had diminished enormously. Suppliers no longer had a guarantee that enterprises would accept their products. Furthermore enterprises were demanding inputs of higher quality than had been delivered in the past. The power of buyers of the companies' products had, however, risen substantially. Enterprises were eager (one might say desperate) to sell their products (even for barter). Purchasers, however, were now able to choose between numerous competing products. The development of product markets had reversed the situation, which had obtained under the command economy, when conditions of shortage were normal and all output found ready buyers.

The local government authorities also seemed to have been losers, insofar as they now had to take on many of the social functions, which had been previously carried out by the enterprises. As enterprises shed their social activities such as housing and recreational facilities, it appeared that the local government authorities had not only lost considerable influence over the enterprise but had had to assume many of their former social responsibilities.

Within the companies themselves the balance of power had also shifted. Power held by external organizations such as the Ministry, Communist Party and trades union, had transferred to the hands of the internal stakeholders. There had also been a transfer of power between departments, from purchasing, production and R&D to newly established or upgraded departments of sales and marketing, accounts and finance and quality.

Most significant, however, has been the shift of power with regard to the workforce and management. Previously, the workforce had enjoyed relatively little power in spite of the official ideology. While many workers have become shareholders of the companies in which they work, this has so far been regarded as a purely nominal position as the vast majority of workers have seen little or no tangible benefit from this. Workers are more likely to think of what they have lost in the transition. The stability and security of employment have vanished. Wages are often paid with considerable delay. The formerly available range of social benefits – from housing to holidays – have to all intents and purposes disappeared. The trades union, moreover, while still in existence, is but a pale shadow of its former self.

The main beneficiaries of the transition have clearly been managers, both senior and middle managers. Middle managers have benefited from the demise – or decline – of external stakeholders such as the Ministry, Communist Party and the trades union. They now enjoy substantial power and control over the workforce, as well as possibly participating in a share of ownership of the company. Middle managers have also gained from widening wage differentials. Some middle managers also have the opportunity of finding work elsewhere (and earning even more). Only those middle managers who can no longer perform adequately under the new circumstances may be in danger of losing their positions.

Senior managers enjoy many of the benefits of increased power as do middle managers; however, to a far greater degree. Many senior managers act and behave as owners of the enterprise. Many have acquired a substantial proportion of the company's shares, which allows them to behave in this way. Ownership and control of the enterprise provide these senior managers with a golden opportunity to demonstrate their expertise, earn high salaries and become wealthy. As in the vast majority of cases external shareholders are in no position to wield significant power, the power of senior managers may appear, and sometimes is, absolute.

9 The Practice and Experience of *Bizness*

INTRODUCTION

In this chapter we now bring together the various issues and strands identified in the contextual and case study chapters, in order to present an integrated picture of how the transformation of the economic and political systems has had an impact on the practice and conduct of business in Volgograd. The momentous changes of the past decade in the political and economic spheres have overturned the former system of economic management, both at the national level and at the level of individual companies. How have individual enterprises and their managers responded to these changes? What are the main issues facing managers under the new circumstances being created by the establishment of a market economy?

SURVIVAL AND MORE

Enterprises which were formerly state-owned have displayed considerable resilience in continuing to survive. Certainly their survival has been abetted by the inefficiency of bankruptcy legislation, continuing support from the public purse at federal and local levels and a political desire to contain unemployment. Enterprises have closed, and these have not necessarily been the least efficient and least advanced (for example, the Volgograd enterprise Avrora which had around 7000 employees, many of whom had been highly qualified scientific personnel. Avrora produced ceramic plates for the space industry; conversion of its production for civilian purposes had allegedly been blocked by Western competitors reluctant to accept new entrants to the industry.) In spite of enterprise closures production continues in the premises of many of these enterprises as small groups work on manufacturing items for which there is manifest demand and payment is normally in cash. Such 'piggy-backing' activities (they 'piggy-back' on the resources of the main enterprise) are also widespread in enterprises which are still operating normally (more or less).

It is thus important to distinguish between the traditional core activities of the enterprise which may be experiencing substantial difficulties with regard to quality and customers and these 'piggy-backing' activities which seem to fulfil a genuine market demand. It therefore appears likely that actual levels of economic activity are far higher than those reported by the enterprises themselves, and unregistered activities comprise the industrial production of goods as well as the more traditional area of services.

Enterprises, moreover, have invested considerable time and effort in evaluating their products, developing new ones and in identifying markets for their products. In the general context of economic uncertainty and, in some respects, ignorance, enterprises have moved from a situation where they were fundamentally production units instructed to deliver a certain volume of outputs and with minimal concern for demand. Enterprises are now fully aware of the need to find customers for their products, as without customers products accumulate at the plant! Managers have thus begun to develop a clear understanding of the relationship between supply and demand, and of the impact this has on the functioning of the company. This is particularly evident in those companies supplying consumer products.

A further area of intense activity has been in restructuring the enterprise. On the one hand enterprises have divested themselves of the political and also of many social functions, and managers tend to focus clearly on the core areas of business activity.

On the other hand, enterprises have also had to take on board a number of functions previously carried out by external bodies such as the relevant industrial ministry. A most obvious manifestation of this has been in the establishment of sales and marketing departments which previously, where they existed, tended to be rudimentary. Other areas of development have been in accounting and finance, quality and public relations. Some managers explained the difference with reference to Western textbook descriptions of organizational structures. Certainly the structure of enterprises now approximates more closely to practice in traditional capitalist economies, even though the content of the work undertaken in the 'new' departments may not necessarily have changed so substantially.

Managers, especially senior managers, have acquired substantial new knowledge and skills and have considerable opportunities to apply them. However, the application of this new learning can be problematical because of the relative inexperience of the learners and the context in which the new learning has to be transferred. However, there is no doubting the enormous willingness to learn among managers, as well as a realization of the need to operate differently by employees.

INDEBTEDNESS AND LIQUIDITY

A general problem of conducting business legally in Russia is mutual indebtedness and the related issue of limited liquidity. Basically, enterprises are both substantial creditors and debtors. Credits and debits have accumulated since the change in economic policy, with the result that mutual indebtedness is both of gigantic dimensions and an intractable problem. The intractable nature of the problem increases with the size of the enterprise. In an efficiently operating market debits and credits are regularly cleared. Uncleared debits tend to lead to bankruptcy and the disappearance from economic activity of any company unable to meet its obligations.

In Russia companies frequently owe and at the same time are owed substantial sums of money (note the mutual indebtedness of the Parts Plant and the Tractor Plant; another company we surveyed was allegedly owed US$15 million and owed US$5 million. This company 'resolved' its problem by getting one of its debtors to stand as guarantor for a substantial bank loan. The managing director admitted that the company would default on the loan, obtaining in this way the money it was due.)

However, there is often little interest in calling in debts as this would in general run counter to the company's own interests. Mutual indebtedness is similar to a pack of cards. If too many debts are called in, and too many companies go bankrupt, the entire system as it is currently constituted is likely to collapse. As few companies are in a position to settle their debts, companies tolerate the current condition of indebtedness out of mutual self-interest. If debts were called in, even potentially profitable companies could go to the wall. Clearly, size is also a consideration in this calculation. Calling in debts is not the same as actually receiving them. The larger the debt, the less willingness to lose the money owed, even if the loss would be only notional. The larger the company, the less likely that bankruptcy would be acceptable politically and socially.

The problem of mutual indebtedness is in large part due to the general lack of liquidity in the economy. There are, however, other manifestations of this lack of liquidity. One aspect is the inability of enterprises to pay wages and salaries in cash, either at all or only with substantial delays. This problem of non-payment of wages and salaries affects both the private and public sectors. Even the federal government is unable to guarantee the payment of wages to public sector employees such as teachers, for the federal government is in no better a position than the companies to ensure payment of taxes in money. In fact, 'real' money accounts for only a quarter of taxes paid. As the Russian deputy Yavlinsky commented: 'The budget now includes condensed milk and tractors' (*Moskovskie Novosti*, no. 38, September 1997:7). According to this article 44 per cent of payments to the federal coffers were in the form of goods, with a further 32 per cent consisting of promissory notes.

The lack of liquidity encourages companies to undertake or permit the undertaking of economic activities for cash. It is likely that many 'piggy-backing' activities operate on this basis. The extent to which such activities enter the realm of the illegal and criminal is difficult to assess. Cash, however, is a scarce commodity. According to one of our interviewees, plastic (i.e. credit cards) represented legal money, while cash was often illegal.

Limited liquidity has also led to the expansion of another phenomenon: barter. Barter played a significant role in East–West trade but was no more than a minor aspect of the economies of Western and former communist trading partners. Sales of a company's products are often on the basis of barter, and companies will offer substantial discounts for payments in cash.

Barter is generally considered a phenomenon of primitive, pre-cash economies. In the Russian context barter has become extensive and developed. The yard of the Parts Plant contained machinery (tractors and construction equipment) received as payment for the company's goods. One piece of construction equipment was to be given to a building company, which was at the time reconstructing the roof of one of the workshops.

The circulation of barter items is not normally so straightforward and barter specialists intervene to facilitate the movement of goods and money within the economic system. Barter specialists negotiate with a number of organizations to resolve 'bottlenecks'. To take a simple imaginary example, a manufacturing company is threatened with the termination of its energy supply, if it does not clear its debts with the energy supplier. The energy supplier is likely to owe at least a similar amount in taxes to the government. The government likewise owes money to public sector organizations. To resolve this situation, the manufacturing company will call in the services of a barter specialist. The barter specialist will negotiate with the energy supplier and the government. The energy supplier will be pleased to see the manufacturing company clear its debt (it will consequently continue selling energy to this company) and to have part of its debt to the government cleared. The government in its turn will be pleased to receive payment, even possibly at a discount, and even if the money goes directly to the government agency (who also will be more than pleased to receive most, if not all, of what is owed).

The barter specialist in the meantime takes goods from the manufacturing company which is enabled to maintain production because of the continuation of energy supplies. The barter specialist converts the company's goods into cash (possibly through a series of exchanges) or into quasi-cash (e.g. foodstuffs to be used for paying employees' wages). The cash goes to the government agency and the barter specialist takes a percentage as his fee.

In general the process of negotiating deals is intricate and depends on having numerous contacts. Only personal contacts tend to be entrusted with carrying out barter deals. In the process of negotiation the palms of the various parts of the chain will have to be greased.

Barter specialists are a symptom of the difficulties being experienced by companies and the economy. Without them, however, there would be even less activity and movement. Barter alleviates some of the current difficulties facing companies but in itself does not represent a long-term solution.

RETAILING

A further response to the general lack of liquidity is companies' involvement in retailing. The First Milk Company's forward integration into retailing gives it direct access to the cash paid by consumers for its products. The movement of the Parts Plant into retailing has a similarly overt rationale.

The Parts Plant has a modern retail outlet adjacent to the plant on one of Volgograd's main thoroughfares. However, the retail outlet does not sell primarily the company's own products but smaller items received in barter (e.g., small agricultural equipment, bicycles, etc.) and articles for personal consumption such as cigarettes and vodka. Items in the retail outlet are sold only for cash.

Companies consequently have recourse to a number of mechanisms to alleviate the problems of low liquidity and mutual indebtedness. It could be argued, however, that barter and retailing in fact detract from the core activities of these organizations. Rather than expending considerable energy in conducting barter deals and establishing retail operations, companies ought to focus on raising efficiency and improving their products and production processes. However, in the relative absence of cash (or credible substitutes) companies would not be able to function at all without their barter, retailing and other cash-generating activities.

THE LABOUR FORCE

Labour forces have been at the cutting edge of the transformation as the former policy of full employment was abandoned. As large enterprises closed or slimmed down, all categories of employees were affected. The closure or 'downsizing' of former military establishments released large numbers of highly qualified scientific workers on to the labour market.

Unemployment hit many individuals profoundly as they were struck by a condition which for them had not previously existed. The response of some employees when they were informed that they no longer had a job was to fall prey to hysteria. The shock of unemployment has a far more profound significance in Russia than in the West, as enterprises provide a wider range of benefits including accommodation. Under communism one's identity was closely linked to the enterprise where one worked.

The pressure on the workforce is likely to continue as enterprises seek to achieve greater efficiency and match output to staffing levels. The managers we interviewed often referred to the poor level of price competitiveness of their companies' products. Locally produced yoghurts were not necessarily cheaper than foreign yoghurts, which had been transported over long distances. The cost of producing basic items such as nuts and bolts was far higher in Volgograd than in other countries. The need to operate efficiently and become internationally competitive will force enterprises to review their current cost structures and review continuously the number of people that are employed.

Not surprisingly, workforces are generally demotivated. Even if they are still employed they cannot but be aware of the critical conditions in which many companies find themselves. The fear of unemployment has become a looming reality. In such a situation it is not clear whether productivity has improved in anything more than a statistical sense, i.e. the figures in the equation have changed, but qualitatively (in terms of attitudes and skill levels) little may have changed.

Ordinary employees, moreover, tend to lack forms of collective organization and protection as the trades unions have become to all intents and purposes powerless. Trades union officials have in some instances become a part of company personnel departments and hence primarily representatives of company interests. At best the trades union can monitor the implementation of legislation and try to ensure that employees are not dismissed in an illegal manner.

The condition of individual workers is in a certain sense paradoxical in that many are both employees and shareholders of the company. However, employee shareholding does not seem to have necessarily strengthened the position of employees within enterprises as many employees do not appear to attach significant value to shares, as in the current circumstances many have yet to receive a dividend from their shareholding. The value of shares resides largely in their sale value, as company managers are often keen to increase the proportion of shares they own. In some cases there is a vibrant external demand for the company's shares (we were told in more than one company that employees were being offered 5 to 6 times the nominal value of the shares by external buyers). Shareholding in fact has strengthened the power of the majority shareholders who are frequently the senior management team.

What is developing in many enterprises is a kind of paternalism where employees look to the managing director to safeguard their interests (in spite of the experience of extensive demanning) and where the senior management team continues to feel a genuine responsibility towards the body of employees (although 'forced' to implement massive cuts in the workforce).

In spite of the substantial decline in employment in former state-owned enterprises, registered unemployment in Volgograd remains remarkably low. What has happened to those employees who have left traditional enterprises? Some have gone into retirement, some have emigrated from the area. However, the majority seem to have found employment elsewhere. Although demand for labour in former state-owned enterprises has fallen dramatically, enterprises still have vacancies for some specialist staff. Other specialists, dissatisfied with lack of opportunities and low salaries in enterprises or the public sector, have become self-employed and engage in a range of services such as barter and trade. The massive expansion of retailing and other services has also provided new employment opportunities. There is also evidence of some movement from the top echelons of former state-owned enterprises into senior positions within the municipal and oblast administrations.

Additional employment opportunities have arisen from unregistered work (for example, working as unlicensed taxi drivers) and criminal activities. Although it is difficult to estimate the scale of these activities, they are clearly substantial and have a greater potential to flourish under the present system of law and order than they enjoyed previously under a system using more rigorous and widespread means of surveillance.

A further source of income generation has been in multiple employment. It is not unusual for individuals to have more than one job, even several jobs, in order to achieve what they consider to be an adequate income. In some cases supplementary income may come from small-scale activities such as growing fruit and vegetables on a smallholding and selling it at the roadside. In other cases individuals may be engaged in a number of parallel activities which are each substantial in their own right. It is, however, difficult to establish the precise contours of such activities as individuals are reluctant to disclose how much they earn overall.

PRODUCT AND PROCESS DEVELOPMENT

Companies are attempting to improve all aspects of their value chains (Porter, 1985). A major problem, however, has been the need to address all aspects of the value chain simultaneously. As well as reducing the labour force and seeking to raise labour productivity, companies have set up human resource departments (in contrast to the former largely administrative personnel departments). In order to achieve sales some companies have also established sales forces and begun to undertake on the whole largely rudimentary forms of marketing. In accounting and finance too, because of the new pressure on companies to generate and account for their own income, accounting and finance departments have been established and exercise a vital function. Furthermore, a desire to improve the R&D and technological base of companies has been hampered in many instances by the lack of resources available to invest in such activities and purchases. Perhaps above all enterprises have had to come to terms with the fact that their products were of low quality and had a poor price–quality relationship when compared with the products of international competitors. Even in the production of simple products such as nuts and bolts the products may fail to meet accepted international standards, or in order to achieve a required volume of output wastage rates may be enormous (at the Parts Plant it required the manufacture of twice the quantity ordered in order to supply items of the requisite quality).

Companies have accordingly come to appreciate that they need to raise the quality of their products and of their production processes. There is evidence that overall product quality is being improved with some consumer products (e.g. chocolate) which are now better packaged than they ever were in the past. Upgrading of processes is also being tackled, but generally requires investment in new machinery, which many enterprises cannot afford to purchase.

Enterprises are clearly paying greater attention to standards, establishing quality departments and seeking to achieve a range of international certifications such as ISO 9000 and ISO 14000. This often involves management and workforce in learning about quality issues. An underlying aim of product and process development is to improve resource allocation by cutting down on the use and wastage of inputs, employing labour more efficiently and manufacturing products which customers want to buy at a price, which allows the company to earn a profit. In so doing, companies are beginning to give up the wasteful approaches of the past, when economic aspects of production were in reality only a secondary consideration. For example, one of our companies was delighted to win an order for its products from Iran, but only subsequently realized the cost involved in producing wooden boxes for the transportation.

Overall, however, there are indications that both product and process quality are improving, even though there is possibly too much trust placed in the value of international certifications, which may become ends in themselves. However, that being said, it appears that managers at least are learning to appreciate that quality is a significant issue and the process of preparing for these international certifications is raising awareness and knowledge of setting and achieving international quality standards.

A major difficulty, however, is in achieving an integration of the various developments taking part throughout the enterprise in the different segments of the value chain. This integration is particularly

difficult in those enterprises with a low volume of sales (and consequently) revenue in proportion to their current size. Only those
companies which are independently profitable (for example, the First
Milk Company) are in a position to take such an integrated approach
and focus their attention on specific components of the value chain
with a view to increasing profit margins further. This capability,
however, widens the gap between successful companies and those
struggling to find a way out of their critical circumstances.

FOREIGN PARTNERS

Foreign direct investment has made little impact on the economy of
Volgograd and its oblast. Certainly the area has been opened up to
foreign products, especially consumer products; conversely local
products now have direct access in the vast majority of cases to
foreign markets (military production is the major exception to this
rule). However, the volume and intensity of exchanges with other
countries appears limited and not always to the benefit of the local
economy. In consumer goods such as tobacco and alcohol foreign
brands are widespread and in many cases priced similarly to local
products. On the other hand none of the enterprises we investigated
had any substantial foreign trade.

Incidences of FDI were also, to say the least, few and far between,
and trade missions to the area from potential investor countries such
as the US, Germany and the United Kingdom do not appear to have
brought much in the way of tangible investments. The foreign investment which has come into the area is to be found in a small number
of companies in raw materials, agricultural production and soft and
alcoholic drinks.

This low level of FDI is not surprising in view of Volgograd's location, the attractiveness (or lack of attractiveness) of the possibilities
for investment it offers and the widespread perception of political
instability in the country held by potential investors. The area does not
appear to have a particular competitive advantage which it can exploit
to attract foreign investors, who may have multiple other locations
from which to choose.

The hopes placed by company managements and local politicians in
the potential of foreign investors seem accordingly misplaced, especially with regard to investment in company restructuring and
revitalization. In some areas such as consumer products, foreign

companies are bringing in new practices and knowledge which may be transferred to other sectors of the economy. However, most companies require much more than this. Role models may provide new ideas and insights. However, the majority of companies need tangible investments.

A further disincentive for foreign investors is the reluctance of many Russians to invest in their economy, and their preference of exporting their savings overseas. As many managers in the survey mentioned, any foreign investment would most likely be misappropriated, for example to pay off debts, rather than be used to restructure and modernize the enterprise. There are therefore substantial grounds for foreign investors to be very cautious in selecting partners and, once selected, monitoring subsequent operations.

OWNERSHIP

The privatization process was implemented with the express aim of transferring as quickly as possible the vast majority of state property into private hands. Not surprisingly anomalies have arisen, as in the case of agriculture, where privatized farms work land which is still owned by the state.

Furthermore privatization seems to have created a small group of active (not to say, aggressive) capitalists and a large, disparate and mainly passive group of small shareholders, who are normally company employees. The new capitalist elite consists of both company directors and managers and outsider groups such as banks and other financial institutions. On the whole, insider ownership predominates.

One of the major problems associated with insider ownership is that company ownership is intimately linked to control. In such circumstances questions arise as to the overall intentions of the owner–managers, in particular with regard to personal and company interests. There is evidence to suggest that companies are being run in a way that tends to further personal interests. For example, company finance may be used to develop new activities which, as soon as they become independently viable (i.e. profitable) are sold to family members or close friends; or 'piggy-back' activities, operating under the umbrella of the company's resources, generate a private revenue for members of senior management.

This dimension of personal enrichment often goes hand in hand with a determined policy of excluding outside 'interference' in the company and maintaining a majority shareholding. For example, at the First Milk Company, having expanded the number of external shareholders in order to generate funds for investment, the senior management team was keen to re-establish their majority shareholding.

Although in many enterprises a large proportion of the shares are owned by individual employees and former employees, in general they fail to appreciate the significance (and potential) of being a shareholder. One of the explanations for this is that in most cases shares have yet to produce any dividend. Second, employee shareholders are a fragmented group and in the absence of collective organization, for example, by the trades union, are easily controlled and manipulated by enterprise management. The serious economic situation also makes the sale of these shares an attractive proposition, with company management being keen to ensure that these shares are sold to them rather than to outsiders. Furthermore, there is no reason to suppose that outsiders will act any more ethically than insider groups of 'robber barons' (Skidelsky, 1996:89). Both insiders and outsiders share the common purpose of maximizing their own share of formerly state-owned property.

There is obviously a conflict between personal enrichment and company restructuring and modernization, although they are clearly not mutually exclusive. No owner is likely to destroy the company completely if it acts as a source of personal enrichment. However, what happens when this is no longer the case, for example, when the enterprise funds have been used to create and spin off new businesses rather than to restructure the enterprise? Or is the market in this way effecting a more efficient allocation of resources from marginal (or negative) to more lucrative activities? Is the invisible hand of the market directing the actions (albeit illicit or unethical) of managers?

FAMILY AND FRIENDS

The rapid transition from communism to capitalism has created a situation in which economic relationships are neither tried nor trusted. To use Granovetter's (1992) often-quoted term, they are not 'embedded'. New institutions and new commercial practices have yet to establish themselves. There are numerous cases in which trust and property have been abused. In such a general context of uncertainty and apprehension, it is not surprising that family, friends and personal contacts play a significant role. *Gemeinschaft* values, to use the term of the German sociologist Ferdinand Tönnies, predominate.

Such values and relationships were manifest during our investigations (ironically our research would have hardly been possible without them). The manifestation of these relationships took a number of forms. Firstly, the ownership and management of many enterprises were in the hands of a small group consisting of family members and close friends. Second, family contacts in, for example, the public administration can facilitate access to municipal and provincial resources such as still publicly owned commercial property as well as a certain protection from criminal oganizations. In the absence of customary, accepted practices, weak institutional forces and powerful criminal tendencies, a reliance on family and friends is clearly a significant economic resource. In the case of barter, to give another example, company directors understandably deal only with intermediaries whom they personally know and trust.

The area of personal trust and contacts expands, however, beyond the circle of close family and friends. What was particularly noticeable in Volgograd was the extensive network of former Communist Party functionaries who were now active in enterprise managements and the public administration. It is not clear whether they have links with the current Communist Party, or what these links may be. However, these people appear to form a local elite encompassing the economic and political spheres.

A further dimension of personal contacts related to the Cossack culture, which continues to be strong in this part of Russia. Being a Cossack may carry some weight in relationships with other Cossacks.

Personal relationships, both between family members and close friends ('quasi-family') and between 'friends' (relationships based on mutual respect, political affiliation or cultural background), involve mutuality and mutual benefit. Favours given have to be repaid if requested. In certain instances this repayment can involve the payment of bribes (monetary or in goods) to the more powerful partner in the relationship.

Clearly such personal relationships have both positive and negative characteristics. On the positive side they permit the conduct of economic transactions in a climate of relative uncertainty, providing reliable information and access to trustworthy expertise as well as to other resources. On the negative side such relationships can create new forms of dependency and abuses of political and economic power, increasing corruption and undermining the development of an open market economy.

MARKET FORCES

As is evident from previous sections, numerous forces are working to circumvent the overt operation of the market. Individual responses are, however, to a large degree a reaction to the ineffective operation of the market itself. Market systems depend on sound foundations of legal institutions and a monetary system implemented by effective state organs. Clearly, in the Russian context, these aspects are at best only evolving.

First, there has since the mid-1980s been a mass of legislation passed relating to the economy. Law has followed law and decree has followed decree. This constant flow of legislation has been at times frequently amended, at times contradictory. It has often been regarded as impeding rather than assisting the development of a market economy. There is so much legislation and it is often poorly implemented, so that in practice it does not provide a basis of trust for economic action. Accordingly, organizations and individuals have regular recourse to extra-legal activities which they regard as effective. Unfortunately, the popular perception is one of legal inadequacy rather than efficiency and effectiveness.

Second, the monetary system is patently not working. The scale of mutual indebtedness is now so vast that its resolution at the national level will require considerable inventiveness. At the level of the firm the problem is being resolved – at least temporarily – by not paying debits and not receiving credits (they just remain on the company's books), issuing promissory notes or other papers and engaging in barter. In this context the market clearly does not work.

Third, the state in its role as guarantor of the framework of the market economy is ineffective: hence the weakness of the legal and monetary systems. One of the consequences of the current situation is that the national economy consists of a number of market or prospective market economies in varying stages of evolution. Some markets (e.g. consumer goods) are subject to considerable competition, and consumers in this case have considerable choice. These factors have combined to put pressure on companies such as the First Milk Factory to restructure, upgrade and innovate in order to match foreign and other local competitors. In other markets, especially industrial markets, development has been less evident and these markets have been characterized by a decline in sales, output and employment, as well as by limited capability of the enterprise to respond.

Further resistance to the development of competitive markets is evidenced by the desire to recreate monopolies, even in the more competitive markets. This desire expresses itself in anti-competitive behaviour (e.g. restricting supplies) and in vertical integration (e.g. expansion into retailing and special contractual and other relationships with suppliers). Once again, this conduct is understandable in the context of the current economic situation and the recent history of company managements. It is almost as if they wish to recreate the certainties of the former economic system, by controlling suppliers and customers, and creating a monopolistic barrier against competitors. While these aspirations are understandable at the level of individual firms, they are in no way discouraged by the institutional context in which they operate.

BUSINESS AND POLITICS

The close relationship between the local economic and political elites has already been noted. The municipal and provincial administrations have an obvious interest in the activities of the area's major enterprises, especially in the area of employment and social services.

Many social functions (e.g. housing, health, pre-school education) are being dropped by companies and are becoming the concern of the public administration even if there are few or no resources to carry them out. Part of the problem of local administrations is that the relationships between the various levels (federal, regional, provincial and municipal) are firstly not always clear and secondly a source of conflict. The demise of centralization has created a situation in which the non-federal bodies are seeking to gain as much political power as possible. There are consequently numerous disputes between the various levels over power and, more concretely, finances. Some disputes over the allocation and distribution of resources are so bitter and protracted that nobody receives anything.

While most enterprises are now free of the formerly powerful influence of the central ministries, the one major exception is the former military enterprises, which in many cases are still dependent on state orders for their production. Also significant is the continuing influence of the military lobby which can decide the fate of potential export orders. The influence of the military lobby also extends beyond the traditional military enterprises and can affect potential sales of industrial enterprises, which have diversified into military production.

Political power in itself can also be attractive to people in business. Previously there was a certain interchangeability between positions in the political (both party and administrative) and the economic spheres. This still applies to a certain degree today, as senior members of the local administration and deputies of the Duma may come from senior positions in economic organizations. Some company directors may also see political office as a way of extending their economic power, by increasing their range of contacts and gaining privileged access to public contracts and finance. Onc company director claimed to have recouped the costs of his electoral campaign in only 3 days as a member of the provincial parliament.

ENTREPRENEURSHIP

In the new political and economic climate entrepreneurship has mushroomed and has taken a variety of forms and nuances. In Chapter 6 we portrayed the transformation of retailing from a bleak state-controlled system prone to endemic shortages to a dynamic, if somewhat variable, constellation of innumerable providers of goods and services. The general transformation created an opportunity for individuals to engage in trading and retail activities; many individuals gladly seized this opportunity; many were pushed through necessity, because of unemployment or general financial constraint.

Managers of formerly state-owned enterprises too could no longer adhere to the economic practices of the past, and had to become opportunity-seekers, if their enterprises were to undergo a satisfactory transformation and survive.

The new entrepreneurial activities can be classified according to a number of categories. First, there is legal entrepreneurial activity where individuals operate openly and account for their income to the relevant state bodies such as the tax authorities. Second, there is small-scale illegal activity such as operating an unregistered taxi service and carrying out relatively small jobs for cash. The definition becomes somewhat more problematical when applied to the 'piggyback' entrepreneurial activities which operate within existing and, in some cases, even within defunct enterprises, and involve collusion between enterprise managements and the operators of the activity. Clearly such activities, which are intended to defraud the tax authorities, make illicit use of company property by not reimbursing the company for the use of its physical and energy resources and enrich personally the individuals involved, are a long way removed from those of the unlicensed taxi driver who is generally acting solely in order to earn a living for himself and his family.

The third category is that of pure criminal activities which have been given plenty of scope and opportunity by the new environment of ineffective state controls and a general climate of precarious legality. In the absence of state controls criminal groups have seized as much space as they can. In so doing they have created to a degree their own structure and order.

One area in which all three categories have shown substantial entrepreneurism is in relation to the current political structures at all levels (Malle, 1996; Skuratov, 1998). The directors of former state enterprises have maintained and cultivated their relationships with federal and local politicians in order to obtain state funding and other support. As already noted, even directors of new private companies believe that economic benefits can be derived from personal involvement in political activities. Small businesses, moreover, need to liaise and negotiate with the local political establishment for licences and possibly premises.

Regrettably, all too often this interaction with the political authorities degenerates into bribery and corruption, both for large and small firms. Furthermore, this kind of 'entrepreneurial' activity is resource-consuming with regard to both time and money, and represents in a narrow economic sense a poor use of the company's resources. To make matters worse, particularly for small business, companies also have to respond to the attentions of criminal organizations extracting payment for the 'roof' or protection money.

In spite of all these difficulties there is now a very large number of businesses based on entrepreneurial activity. The spirit of entrepreneurism, moreover, appears rather robust. Individuals continue to set up and run businesses notwithstanding the demands of the political authorities and criminal organizations. Individual entrepreneurs too appear rather resilient to failure, which is regarded as an acceptable phenomenon of the contemporary dynamic and unstable circumstances. The response to failure and bankruptcy is generally to start again by founding another new business and, as described in

Chapter 7, 'wise' entrepreneurs tend to have embryo businesses in reserve, to be developed as soon as the situation requires it.

THE SOCIAL SPHERE

The social sphere has been considerably eroded. Enterprises have divested themselves of a substantial proportion of their former social activities. This loss appears regretted by managers and workers alike. The cutbacks have been justified in terms of the economic priorities of the current transformation. At the same time many managers expressed the hope that the social sphere would be revived as soon as the economic circumstances of the enterprise permitted. Furthermore, the municipal and provincial authorities are able, in only the most limited of ways, to compensate for the loss of company-based social services.

Not surprisingly, there has been an upsurge of individualism, as evidenced by the expansion of the legal and illegal entrepreneurial and small business sector. This individualism has in many cases been driven by necessity and, wherever possible, within the context of 'family' relationships.

The sudden shift from collective activities centred on the enterprise has resulted in considerable hardship for those individuals lacking the requisite individual resources (skills, knowledge and state of mind) to undergo the transition with its enormous uncertainties. The former system did not exactly encourage and foster individual initiative and self-reliance.

Somewhat surprisingly, official unemployment is low and the majority of people who have been affected negatively, grumble but often do little more. There is some nostalgia for the past but also an appreciation of the benefits of the present.

The general situation is bleak for many, and unstructured. The future is unclear. Yet in spite of everything there has been relatively little social unrest and the discipline of the past is continuing to hold, at least for the present.

CONCLUSIONS

A range of individual and corporate responses to the transformation can be identified. These responses portray a situation of paradoxes and nuances rather than a black-and-white picture of success and failure. New practices and approaches go hand-in-hand with traditional forms of negotiation and appeal. There is no one way which would seem to guarantee success or at least a way out of the present circumstances. Entrepreneurism is allied to a recourse to traditional practices such as a reliance on personal contacts, favours and bribes. New business opportunities may depend as much on the support of influential political personalities and groups as on the entrepreneurism and newly developed business skills of the business people involved.

Such a combination of the old and the new is not surprising in the Russian context, as 70 years of communism gave way to a capitalism which is imprecisely delineated because of an emerging, and hence generally weak, institutional structure. There is ample evidence of entrepreneurism and new attitudes and practices. There is also ample evidence of the persistence of values, and practices of the former regime. The significance of this duality is one of the themes of our final chapter.

10 Reflections, Conclusions and Prognoses

In this final chapter the authors reflect on their experience of conducting research in Volgograd, so as to draw conclusions from the data they collected and their analysis of it and consider the possible future paths of development for Volgograd and its oblast. The first section of this chapter therefore focuses on the methodological and practical issues of carrying out research in the conditions of contemporary Russia and, more specifically, in the Russian province. This section is followed by the identification and discussion of some general trends (and dichotomies) which have emerged from the research. Finally, the authors explore a number of alternative scenarios for the development of companies and the local economy, even though they are fully aware of the shifting sands on which such an approach in the current economic state of Russia is based.

GATEKEEPERS

As mentioned earlier, our research was greatly facilitated by a number of key individuals who helped us considerably in obtaining access to companies. We are very grateful to these gatekeepers and to those senior and middle managers in our case study and other companies who discussed their work and their problems with us. However, we frequently wondered about the extent to which our image and understanding of the situation in Volgograd was being influenced by these gatekeepers. For example, were we being directed to visit only successful enterprises? Were managers embellishing the situation of their companies, motivated by a 'desire "to present the enterprise in the best possible way to strangers"' (Kiblitskaya, 1995:208).

We countered these concerns in a number of ways. First, whilst being grateful, we felt in no way beholden to our gatekeepers and have sought to present as accurate a picture as possible of what we heard and observed. Second, the composition of the research team provided us with a sound basis for understanding the role of gatekeepers and the behaviour of managers. Third, we collected and compared data from a range of informants and sources. Fourth, managers' portrayals of the situation tended on the whole to be gloomy, emphasizing difficulties of the transformation and the demanding changes in operations and processes which companies and individuals were experiencing. In one company we were invited to a lavish lunch. This was the culmination of a visit to the company's premises which included obsolescent machinery and crumbling workshops. In general, it is difficult to hide the physical conditions of plant and buildings, and there seemed to be no problems in being shown around plants and in being told about their actual conditions.

POTEMKIN

Prince Grigorij Potemkin's claim to fame lies in his policy of deceit. A visit to the Crimea by Catherine the Great in 1787 involved the construction of fictitious villages – mere façades or stage sets for the benefit of the visiting Tsarina to convey a picture of prosperity in a situation of abject poverty. Many of Volgograd's industrial enterprises have become something akin to Potemkinesque villages, albeit in reverse. Factories stretch along the 100 km of ribbon development which is the city of Volgograd. Many of these factories – industrial giants of the past – have now closed or are greatly reduced. Has Volgograd become one large Potemkinesque agglomeration? Clearly such a description is an exaggeration. Not all (or even the majority) of the old large enterprises have closed. Furthermore even enterprises which are officially closed show signs of life and working activity. There is obviously some kind of regeneration and renewal taking place within the remains of defunct industrial dinosaurs.

Such activities (often unregistered) are, however, difficult to 'capture' and difficult to track. They are proactive responses to market needs, generally producing to a specific demand. These operations are on the whole unburdened by the legacy of the past and in many cases by the contemporary legal obligations of conducting business.

The reality of the situation can therefore be discovered only by peeling away the various layers of data and observation. A particular company may have closed – but not all economic activity within it. Another company may be struggling to define and revive its core business and at the same time accommodates comparatively thriving lamprey-like activities. Another company still may break out of its traditional area of operations, diversifying into new product areas or integrating both backward and forward. Potemkin's aim had been to disguise the absence of activity. Even under communism a handsome façade might house a producer of shoddy goods. However, in the current context the aim is often to disguise highly profitable activities and to retain as much of the benefits as possible (often to the detriment of the organization providing the façade).

OPENNESS AND SECRECY

In collecting our data we experienced both openness and secrecy, a willingness to provide data and discuss the current situation and a refusal to talk. Data and information are now widely and freely available. In addition to official sources of information considerable information is disseminated through a largely free and critical press. Many individuals willingly provided us with company data and internal documents.

One problem, however, with all this information, is its reliability, as there are many benefits to be derived from distorting the actual situation – for example, to reduce companies' tax bills. We therefore treated all individual items of data with extreme caution and sought confirmation from alternative sources. In spite of (because of?) the new spirit of openness, data can be as unreliable as it was in the past since the motivation to present a particular version of reality is still widespread.

While in some cases we suffered from a kind of information overload in other – relatively few – instances we were refused access and information. The argument was generally that the topic was too sensitive to be discussed or that the data were not available publicly. To give an example, on one occasion we were refused information on one of the military enterprises, only to subsequently find the data we had requested in the press – provided by the enterprise director in an interview!

There are clearly tensions between the secretive practices of the past and the more recent practices of glasnost. Strangers (and especially foreigners) may be treated with suspicion. At the other extreme individuals' openness may border on indiscretion which could rebound on the individuals concerned. Our aim throughout has been to use the data we have collected, but at the same time protecting individuals from indiscretions (uttered in private).

THROUGH WESTERN EYES

Is there one 'objective' image of the situation in Volgograd? Do British and Russian researchers view the situation in the same way? These and similar questions are difficult to answer. The native researcher has a deeper understanding of local conditions and practices, may be more sensitive to what is said and how things are said and presented. The local researcher will generally be more aware of the 'background noises' relating to data collection. At the same time the local researcher may be so integrated in the situation that he or she fails to recognize certain issues, precisely because they may be so familiar and are taken for granted.

On the other hand, the 'foreign' researcher may bring with him or her an entire baggage of preconceived ideas (and in some cases sheer and utter ignorance) which precludes the 'foreign' researcher from appreciating the context and significance of statements and data. The 'foreign' researcher, in contrast, may bring new insights and new approaches, possibly also a certain novelty value, the indulgence traditionally accorded to fools ('You have travelled 3000 km and haven't come to do business?!').

In our view the heterogeneity of the research team was one of the strengths on which the project was built. The team had a range of strengths and attributes which were used to facilitate the research process. The different backgrounds and experiences of the researchers were helpful in gaining access to a range of data sources, in having a permanent presence in Volgograd, in interpreting the data and in structuring the analysis. Hopefully the interaction has been synergetic, creating an outcome which is greater than that which we might individually have achieved.

MACRO AND MICRO

Under the former communist system of economic management there was a clear linear, vertical relationship between political aims, the central economic plan and the activities of individual enterprises – in theory, at least. The reality at enterprise level often differed from the expectations of planners, but these differences were in general regarded as aberrations of the system rather than inherent in the system itself. Both planners and enterprises strove to achieve plan fulfilment and projected an image of the practical success of central planning.

The present circumstances no longer provide such a clear relationship between the broad lines of economic policy and the decisions and activities of individual companies. Certainly, the political decision to establish a market economy (together with a political democracy) has been taken. However, the disappearance of the command economy and its political superstructure has resulted in a kind of vacuum which is being filled in a rather haphazard way. As discussed in the previous chapter, the fundamental institutions of a market economy – legal and monetary institutions – are still embryonic. Some of the outcomes of such a situation are that: barter operates alongside the monetary system; the state monetary system is furthermore matched by parallel 'monetary' systems operated by companies and local government authorities, for example, in the form of promissory notes; legal dispositions are imperfectly applied – the limited implementation of bankruptcy legislation and the only partial effectiveness of tax collection are examples of this imperfect application.

There are therefore strong incentives for companies to circumvent the rules of the market economy. Non-payment (to workers, suppliers and the tax authorities) is endemic. Companies may try to re-create positions of monopoly. In this they will often be abetted by local government bodies who are keen to safeguard employment and dispel possibilities of social unrest. It is true that this situation does not prevail in all provinces. However, it is also true that only a minority of provinces have thrown themselves wholeheartedly into the creation of an effectively functioning market economy. Furthermore, of the more conservative (i.e. less inclined to foster radical change) Volgograd is by no means the most extreme.

One outcome of this situation is that central decisions on economic policy reach the province in a filtered (one might say diluted) version. The central authorities lack the influence and power needed to impose their will. In the absence of a local elite sympathetic to the aims of the central authorities, the market economy develops in an uneven and distorted fashion. 'Strong' companies play the market game, 'weaker' companies seek to resist and adapt it to their own particular requirements of survival and restructuring. The 'strong' companies are in a position to ignore more or less the ineffectiveness of the central authorities (they too cannot ignore this completely as they are also affected by the inefficiencies of the current system). The 'weaker' companies on the other hand resort to traditional practices of political lobbying, but now largely confined to the local government level.

Many managers, moreover, expressed a sense of regret at the diminished role of state authorities, for example, in providing finance for R&D and technological development. Many managers also continued to look to the state to resolve the current crisis, to save companies from the perilous situations in which they currently find themselves. One frequently bandied solution was for the state to 'wipe the slate clean'.

PAST, PRESENT AND FUTURE

Contemporary Volgograd combines the legacy of the past with intimations of an emerging but as yet not fully defined future. Political affairs are still strongly influenced by the former communist elite, although in Volgograd they appear to be more inclined to come to terms with the present situation than is the case in other areas with a more conservative political stance. There is a certain nostalgia for a more secure and glorious past (One graffiti asked: 'When can we have our Stalingrad back?'). However, nostalgia for the pre-reform days does not appear as a salient theme of people's thinking.

In the economic sphere too, as portrayed in Part II of this book, company managements struggle in varying degrees to make sense of, and learn to operate in, the current circumstances. The legacy of the past affects different categories of company in different ways. The former giants of Soviet industry and the former military enterprises in general carry the heaviest burden of the past – transformation and conversion are difficult and slow. Survival is the major priority and not all of these enterprises have survived. However, enterprise managements have demonstrated considerable ingenuity in surviving for so long in spite of the federal policy of rapid privatization. One explanation for this protracted survival is the slowness of the process of establishing a market economy. The relative absence of effective market institutions gives companies a breathing space in which to restructure and reorientate themselves.

In contrast small businesses and companies in the consumer goods industries present a picture of a potential future consisting of plentiful goods and services. While still carrying elements of the past, this sector of economic activity demonstrates the capacity for renewal and innovation and provides evidence of a genuine entrepreneurship and risk-taking.

Social life is also in a transitional phase. Life as organized by the Communist Party and the employing enterprise has increasingly disappeared. Collective organization of the social sphere has given way more and more to individual pursuits. The traditional social infrastructure of everyday life has crumbled but has yet to disappear completely. Company provision of social facilities such as housing and educational and recreational facilities has declined but has not totally disappeared. For many people loss of employment has meant the loss of the entire social context in which they had lived, as employment signified far more than a mere source of income.

Interestingly, many company managers continue to feel a responsibility to provide their employees with social services. While recognizing the difficulty of providing such services at a time of severe economic constraints, they seem to look forward, genuinely, to a more prosperous future when the company will once again be in a position to provide for its employees more than just a job. Traditional practices of the past thus get projected into the future.

The collective organization of the communist regime has given way to individual liberty and choice. For some this has meant an opportunity to express themselves more freely in the private and economic spheres. For those with the necessary wherewithal life has changed considerably for the better. For many, however, especially those made redundant, but even for those in employment receiving wages in barter and after considerable delays, life is clearly more difficult and insecure. Even many of the beneficiaries of the transformation, whilst enjoying their new status and lifestyle, are visibly concerned by the development of the general situation, with its continuously widening gulf between the haves and the have-nots.

CRIMINALITY AND MORALITY

Volgograd is a fertile ground for a broad spectrum of criminal activity. The former regime was oppressive: it constrained personal initiatives and individual freedom. At the same time the repressiveness of the system tended to hold in check criminal activities as the likelihood of detection and apprehension were high and sentences tended to be draconian. Criminality, including serious crimes such as murder, has been increasing steadily during the decade. The collapse of the communist system, deficiencies in the current system of law enforcement, economic difficulties and, it must be said, new economic opportunities, as well as an overall climate of political instability, have contributed to a climate of rising lawlessness, which appears all the more threatening when contrasted with the seeming social harmony and legality of the pre-reform years. In spite of the dangers of over-exaggeration, criminality is a serious phenomenon of contemporary life. According to the governor of Volgograd oblast, 'criminality today is becoming a real force to be reckoned with, threatening the socio-economic development of the state and its national security' (*Volgogradskaja Pravda*, 23 March 1998).

Economic crime, as previously noted, is also on the increase. Its most common manifestation is tax evasion. The oblast administration estimates that around 80 per cent of registered companies do not pay their taxes in full. This costs the oblast around 3 trillion roubles in lost tax revenue. In addition one has to include tax evasion by unregistered companies and by individuals. A worrying new phenomenon is the cooperation in economic crimes between business organizations and outright criminal structures.

The problems of criminality are exacerbated by ineffective law enforcement and alleged corruption among police officers. Many crimes remain unsolved. A more serious matter, however, is the degree of corruption prevalent among 'public servants', including the police. According to Skuratov (1998:93) over 70 per cent of public officials have been involved in corrupt practices such as taking bribes; business organizations spend between 30 and 50 per cent of their earnings on maintaining special relationships with the state bodies; and up to 40 per cent of loans end up as cash payments in the pockets of all grades of public officials.

Whilst recognizing the scale of criminality and corruption (Russia is widely recognized as a world leader in these areas), there is also evidence of considerable 'moral' behaviour; at times both aspects are embodied in the same individual. This morality may in many cases be restricted to members of one's own family and close friends. However, it also exists in the moral obligations which many enterprise directors and managers feel towards the company's employees. This morality is derived from the traditional collectivist organization of Russian and Soviet society, from the experience of the enterprise as a social as well as an economic entity, from a view of employees which is inherently paternalistic. Many managers would like the enterprise to retain and revive its social functions. Such a version of morality may be derided as being outmoded or inappropriate in a market economy, with its emphasis on individual effort, responsibility and achievement. On the other hand, all of the managers we interviewed spoke only with regret about the number of employees who had been made redundant, and described the pain involved in telling employees that they had to leave the company. The issue is not that the remaining workforce are not being exploited (continuous delayed payment of wages is just one example of this exploitation) but that often moral and immoral (or illicit) behaviours are inextricably linked.

ANOTHER PERSPECTIVE

Can other perspectives help us to understand the current situation in Russia? Which other advanced economies have had in the recent past to undergo a system change? Analogies with Italy appear a possibility. After all, Italy experienced a system change from fascism to democracy in the period 1943–5, although the system change was largely restricted to the political sphere and Mussolini's fascist regime lasted little more than 20 years.

It is, however, possible to identify some parallels between post-war Italy and the current situation in Russia: the existence of highly organized criminal groups (the Mafia); the cultivation of special relationships between the state bureaucracy and various interest groups; and a complex relationship between the political and economic spheres, characterized in Italy's case by 'immobilism of the polity' and 'dynamism of the economy' (Allum, 1973:241).

As noted in the previous section, organized crime is a serious social phenomenon in Russia just as it has been in parts of post-war Italy. A key feature of both countries' criminal organizations has been their ability to operate relatively openly and to resist attempts by the legal authorities to crush their activities.

The second dimension relates to the state administration and its susceptibility to external influences. This involves a two-way relationship in which favours granted by the bureaucracy are exchanged for rewards which may be either tangible or intangible. Allum (1973:107), summarizing LaPalombara, highlights 'the ability to create and maintain fixed channels of access is more important than the ability to exercise pressure through an agency outside the administrative system'. In Chapter 5 we saw that an export licence for military products was blocked by the military–industrial complex, because the company requesting the licence was an outsider and hence a competitor. As in post-war Italy relations of mutual interest and favour between public servants and company representatives are widespread in today's Russia. The parallels between post-war Italy and contemporary Russia have been drawn not so much to identify similarities or provide role models but to provide further insights into the situation in Russia. One observation from the Italian experience is that it is possible to have economic progress even in a situation of 'government beset by instability and delay, contradiction and inefficiency' (Allum, 1973:241).

A further observation is that the current political arrangements need not be permanent, but that change can be a slow process. Today's Italy is different in a number of fundamental ways from the Italy which evolved after the collapse of fascism. The systems of political patronage and organized crime have been publicly exposed and largely rejected. There is a resurgent civic mentality which demands openness and accountability. These civic virtues have taken a long time to mature and assert themselves. In the next section we will take account of some of these issues in exploring alternative scenarios for the future of Russian companies.

SCENARIOS

Scenarios provide an opportunity to explore alternative futures on the basis of pre-specified assumptions. Scenario planning is akin to, although not the same as, forecasting. What does the future hold for the kinds of companies we investigated in Volgograd? As a result of the political and economic reforms, Russia – both politically and economically – is very different from what the Soviet Union had been a decade before. Furthermore, the contemporary situation for companies is very different from what was envisaged by the reformers. In spite of system change and a clear political agenda involving rapid mass privatization and the establishment of a market economy, the situation for companies in Russia has developed in an idiosyncratic way. Companies have in general shown unexpected resilience in adapting to the changed circumstances, in particular to the disappearance of the command economy and central planning, and have been able to counteract the influence of the emerging market institutions.

Other researchers, for example Yergin and Gustafson (1993), have already sought to identify the main alternatives for Russia's development up to the year 2010. Yergin and Gustafson (1993) propose four alternative scenarios: a combination of past legacies and future developments; a disintegration of the federal state; military dictatorship; and an economic miracle. These scenarios are not necessarily mutually exclusive and are far more ambitious in scope and time-scale than the scenarios for companies that we will propose. One of our assumptions is that there will not be a return to communism and the command economy. However ineffectual the economic reforms, too much water has passed under the bridge since central planning came to an end. Furthermore, there is now a substantial class of Russian capitalists with a vested interest in resisting any such move.

A second assumption is that the presidential elections of the year 2000 will be highly influential. Yeltsin has demonstrated that the role of president is not only crucial, but extremely powerful. The course of events in Russia will clearly be determined to a large degree by the person who is elected president in 2000. Thus while changes may take a long time to become established, the direction of change may be significantly affected by events such as the inauguration of a new president.

SCENARIO 1: CONTINUATION OF THE PRESENT

The first scenario assumes that the general environmental conditions will continue to be very much as at present. The political scene will remain fragmented, with the centre and regions still locked in battle over respective shares of authority and power. The centre will be important as a guarantor of the general lines of development of the state and the economy, that is, political democracy and a free market. However, the centre's authority will extend only in a limited degree to the regions and provinces. At local level coalitions between local administrations and leading enterprises will still be significant. So long as social stability prevails, this scenario may be maintained. Public administrations will support local companies by means of a protectionist ordering policy – the needs of the public administration will be met by local firms. The consolidation of regional economies, because of local protectionist policies and the cost of long-distance transportation, will further contribute to the maintenance of the status quo.

A key issue remains inter-company indebtedness. Provided the organizations involved in mutual indebtedness are prepared not to demand the repayment of debts, provided the intricate web of mutual obligations remains intact, then companies will tend to behave as they have hitherto. Without the threat of bankruptcy company managements will on the whole continue to prefer the widespread current practice of personal enrichment to the detriment of company restructuring and renewal. The 'perverse behaviours' of former state-owned companies – delayed payment of employees' wages, non-monetary forms of exchange and limited innovation – will persist (Rutland, 1996) in spite of the danger of a 'vicious circle of decline' (*ibid.*).

At the same time more proactive companies (for example, small businesses and consumer-based companies such as the First Milk Company) will continue to thrive, but occupying particular segments of the economy. Larger companies will seek to establish and maintain monopoly positions. Smaller companies will succeed or fail depending on their responsiveness to market demands and on their links with the public administrations. The birth and death rates of SMEs will continue to be high, because the space available for their activities will continue to be limited, as larger companies continue with policies of self-sufficiency and strive to carry out as many of their activities as possible within the firm rather than sub-contracting them to small organizations.

If this scenario of limited change is realized, barter will keep its significant role as the lubricant of the economic system. This will indicate, however, that the monetary system will have stalled and that companies will have failed to find sufficient customers to pay for their products in liquid currency. The reliance on barter, moreover, will slow down the processes of company activities, including regeneration. The outcome of this scenario is likely to be ongoing stagnation, reliance on a closed local economy and increased detachment from the global economy, since companies' products will fall more and more behind those of international competitors.

SCENARIO 2: REVIVAL

The 'revival' scenario requires rose-tinted spectacles. It is predicated on two broad assumptions at the macro and micro levels. At the macro level the scenario presupposes that the state, possibly after the next presidential elections, is able to stabilize the relationship between centre and regions and push forward the development of effective market institutions. If this were to happen, confidence in the market economy would probably rise, with increased willingness on the part of domestic and foreign investors to risk more of their capital in Russian companies. At the same time mutual indebtedness would begin to unblock, as the free circulation of 'liquid' currency would obviate the need for non-payment. Companies would either pay or go to the wall, causing a significant shake-out within industries and increasing competition. The attraction of cash returns will also encourage shareholders (many of whom have been up till now rather passive) to take a greater interest in their shareholdings and the activities of their companies. All in all these developments at the macro level will increase the pressure on companies to operate cost-effectively and to meet market demands. There will therefore be an increasing need for companies to invest in product innovation and development and to raise the quality of their processes and technology.

At the local level there is an opportunity for companies to capitalize on the strengths of Volgograd, its province and other contiguous areas. In the first instance companies could begin to exploit (or exploit more effectively) the natural resources of the area. These include both mineral resources such as petroleum and agricultural potential. Volgograd province already produces a range of agricultural products which are considered of good quality. These products (for example, tomatoes and sunflowers) could regenerate and expand the local food-processing industry. Such a revitalization of agricultural production, with its concomitant benefits for the so-called 'agro-industrial complex', would also spill over positively into industrial production in Volgograd in companies such as the Tractor Plant and its suppliers. A key issue in such a scenario would be to provide the incentives and resources to encourage farmers to upgrade their technology and processes.

A major contributory element to the realization of the 'revival' scenario is the availability of skilled, in some instances highly skilled, labour in Volgograd. The continuing decline in the activities and dimensions of former military enterprises (former concentrations of highly skilled professionals) will release on to the labour market even more employees for other companies. An appropriate utilization of these resources could help to underpin the regeneration of local agriculture and industry, especially in a climate which is conducive to such a regeneration.

The final plank in the 'revival' scenario is the exploitation of Volgograd's strategic geographical position. Volgograd could develop into a significant hub for communications not only in southern Russia, but a considerable international hub linking southern Russia to the

Ukraine, Kazakhstan, the republics of the Caucasus and beyond. There may therefore be considerable potential in Volgograd becoming a gateway not only to the nearby former Soviet republics but also the entire Near and Middle East regions.

SCENARIO 3: A RUSSIAN COMPROMISE

The final scenario presupposes that neither of the first two scenarios will actually be realized, but that the outcome will be some kind of messy combination of the two. Both at the macro and micro levels there will be some positive developments. However, the inertia of the system and vested interests will tend to maintain the status quo, although there will be a slow movement in the direction of effective market institutions and more efficient firms. On the whole, however, the political priority both in the centre and the regions will be to maintain the current disposition of the 'pack of cards'. There will be a fear that if any one card is dislodged, the whole edifice will crumble. The close ties between company directors and public administrators and politicians will help to maintain this situation.

This scenario differs from the first scenario in that there will be attempts to adapt to change, but these adaptations will be fragmented and disjointed and will not address the major general issues of the establishment of a market economy. A key factor in this scenario is the desire of the new Russian capitalists to consolidate their positions, but in a context of limited competition and outsider intervention.

A more positive interpretation of this scenario foresees a more substantial movement towards a market economy, with existing networks of influence acting as a safeguard against the 'excesses' of the market. Political contacts will be used to ward off 'excessive' competition, influence political decision-making and gain preferential access to public contracts. This cooperation between the private and public spheres will bring both benefits and disadvantages. It may permit a certain renewal of companies and a certain expansion of economic activity, but on the whole it is unlikely to complete an effective transformation process. A key question will be the ability of such an approach to maintain social stability. However, this scenario is hardly likely to enhance Volgograd's attractiveness to new investors.

CONTINUITY AND CHANGE

The complexity of the Russian situation and the difficulty of identifying the contours of future developments makes scenario planning highly problematic. The overall political and economic system is as yet not particularly robust and therefore single events – such as the election of a new president – could have a major influence on future developments.

In our research in Volgograd we have noticed the ability of individuals and their companies to be positive about change, to be innovative and entrepreneurial. At the same time we have also noticed a desire to resist change, to adapt in small ways rather than make radical changes. The words of Aleksandr Yakovlev, former advisor to President Gorbachev, still ring largely true today: 'The conservatism that has eaten into everyone and into society, like rust, has turned out to be more durable than we expected.... Resistance to change has turned out to be very strong' (Smith, 1990:558). This tension between change and continuity is one of the main features of economic life in Russia today. In spite of the substantial resistance to change, change is occurring and is making itself felt. Many managers and their companies may, however, have exhausted the greater part of their energies on resisting change rather than on meeting the challenge of a new way of organizing and managing enterprise.

Postscript

The manuscript was completed in late May 1998. In August 1998 Russia gave further proof of the unpredictability of the situation in the country. The decision of the Kirienko government of 17 August 1998, to cease respecting Russian debt obligations to foreign and domestic lenders, created a deep financial, economic and political crisis. The value of the rouble, compared to the dollar, fell by two thirds and has continued falling. As a result real average wages fell by 34.8 per cent (*Izvestia*, no. 233, 11 December 1998). Annual inflation is expected to be at least 50–60 per cent in 1999.

One of the authors experienced the crisis at first hand. The other two authors have revisited the Russian province since the summer, making visits to both Volgograd in November 1998 and Novgorod (see p. 45) in December 1998. The general mood of the people with whom we spoke is one of shock and despair. For many people the gains made since 1992 have been utterly dissipated. At the same time, a construction company in Novgorod was having little difficulty in finding buyers for its small apartments costing US$50,000. The impact of the recent crisis thus appears to have hit people disproportionately, widening the gap between the 'haves' and the 'have-nots'. Those with assets, particularly assets in US dollars and similar currencies, have in many ways benefited from the huge devaluation of the rouble. Those dependent on wages, salaries and pensions in roubles are having to come to terms with considerably higher prices for food, rent and energy.

This situation of crisis and despair is compounded by the apparent inability of the country's political elite to deal with the crisis and propose credible solutions. This political inertia fuels the feeling of nostalgia for the stability of the past. The challenges facing Russian managers and their companies remain, however, basically the same as those described in the chapters of this book.

In fact, all the negative tendencies analysed in the book have become even more apparent. Russian industries, with the small exception of those exporting products and having rouble costs and hard currency revenues, are in even deeper crisis. The decline of GDP is estimated to be a further 6 per cent in 1999. There is still no transparent tax code, and tax collection resembles a dangerous adventure.

Small business and the retail trade are among the hardest hit. The long-awaited land reform, which was supposed to allow real private ownership of land (and which has been under discussion for the past five years), was rejected by the Duma on 23 December 1998. Relations between Russia's regions and the centre deteriorated even further, provoking a series of publications in the central press, asking the key question whether the Russian Federation will survive beyond spring 1999. The budget deficit is growing, and overall Russia's external debt is more than US$150 billion, with the first US$17.5 billion due for repayment in 1999. Given the huge pressures of finding cash to pay wages and salaries, the Primakov government initiated the so-called 'controlled' issue of money. There is the obvious danger that this measure could recreate the hyperinflation of 1992. If this happens, the country will not only be thrown back in time to the first year of the reform, but there could be unforeseen and disastrous consequences.

December 1998

References

ABC (1997), *The Basics of Doing Business in ... Volgograd, Russia* (Volgograd: American Business Centre).

Agapsov, S. (1997), *Promyshlennoe predpriatie v rynochnoj ekonomike: opyt vyzhivania* (Volgograd: Peremena).

Allum, P. (1973), *Italy – Republic without Government?* (London: Weidenfeld & Nicolson).

Angressano, J. (1992), *Comparative Economics* (Hemel Hempstead: Prentice Hall).

Argumenty i Fakty (St Petersburg, weekly).

Astapovich, A. (1995), *Inostrannye Investicii v Rossii* (Moscow).

Barnes, M. and Sansome, G. (1996), *Russian Agriculture: Volgograd and Rostov Regions* (London: Ministry of Agriculture, Fisheries and Food).

Barrikady (1989), *Nizhnee Povolzhie* (Volgograd).

Bim, A. (1996), 'Ownership and Control of Enterprises', *Communist Economies and Economic Transformation*, 8:4, pp. 471–500.

Birman, I. (1996), 'Gloomy Prospects for the Russian Economy', *Europe–Asia Studies*, 48:5, pp. 735–50.

Boyko, M., Shleifer, A. and Vishny, R. (1995), *Privatizing Russia* (Cambridge, MA: MIT Press).

Brock, G. (1994), 'Agricultural Productivity in Volgograd Province', *Comparative Economic Studies*, 36:1, pp. 33–53.

Chamberlain, L. (1995), *Volga, Volga: A Voyage down the Great River* (London and Basingstoke: Picador).

Clarke, S. (1996), 'The Enterprise in the Era of Transition', in S. Clarke (ed.), *The Russian Enterprise in Transition* (Cheltenham: Edward Elgar) pp. 1–61.

Deloviye vesti (Volgograd, weekly).

Delovoye Povolzhie (Volgograd, weekly).

Dmitriev, Y. (1996), *Maly Biznes: faktory i mechanizmy regulirovania* (Volgograd).

Dolgov, M. (1993), 'Maly biznes i nalogi', *Ekonomika i zhizn'*, no. 3.

Dubova, M. (1997), *Ekonomika Regiona* (Volgograd).

Dyker, A. (1992), *Restructuring the Soviet Economy* (London and New York: Routledge).

Ekonomika i zhizn (Moscow, monthly).

Ekonomist (Moscow, monthly).

Ellman, M. (1993), 'General Aspects of Transition', in Ellman, M., Gaidar, E. T. and Kolodko, G. W. (eds), *Economic Transition in Eastern Europe* (Cambridge, MA and Oxford: Blackwell) pp. 1–42.

Ernst, M., Alexeev, M. and Marer, P. (1996), *Transforming the Core* (Oxford: Westview Press).

Finansovye izvestia (Moscow, weekly).

Finansy (Moscow, monthly).

Frydman, R. and Rapaczynski, A. (1994), *Privatization in Eastern Europe:*

Is the State Withering Away? (London: Central European University Press).

Gaddy, C. G. (1996), *The Price of the Past* (Washington, DC: Brookings Institution Press).

Golikova, V. and Avilova, A. (1997), 'State Support for the Development of Small Business in the Russian Region', *Communist Economies and Economic Transformation*, 9:4, pp. 423–31.

Goskomstat (1996), *Socialnoe polozhenie semej, detej, podrostkov: Perspektivy i sovremennost* (Volgograd).

Goskomstat (1997), *Socialnoe polozhenie semej, detej, podrostkov: Perspektivy i sovremennost* (Volgograd).

Granovetter, M. (1992), 'Economic Action and Social Structure: The Problem of Embeddedness', in Granovetter, M. and Swedberg, R. (eds), *The Sociology of Economic Life* (Boulder, CO: Westview Press), pp. 53–81.

Gregory, P. and Stuart, R. (1990), *Soviet Economic Performance* (London: Harper Collins).

Holsti, O. (1969), *Content Analysis for the Social Sciences and Humanities* (Reading, MA: Addison Wesley).

Inter (Volgograd, weekly).

Izvestia (Moscow, daily).

Johnson, G. and Scholes, K. (1997), *Exploring Corporate Strategy* (Hemel Hempstead: Prentice Hall, 4th edn).

Kiblitskaya, M. (1995), 'We Didn't Make the Plan', in S. Clarke (ed.), *Management and Industry in Russia* (Cheltenham: Edward Elgar) pp. 198–223.

Kornai, J. (1990), *The Socialist System* (Princeton, NJ: Princeton University Press).

Kotz, D. and Weir, F. (1997), *The Revolution from Above* (London and New York: Routledge).

Ksenofontova, N., Ustinov, G. and Shutkin, A. (1996), 'Efektivnost ispolzovania gosudarstvennych sredstv v malom predprijatii', *Financy*, 6, pp. 15–20.

Lavigne, M. (1995), *The Economics of Transition* (Basingstoke and London: Macmillan).

Lavrov, A. (1998), 'Problems of Inter-Budgetary Relations in the Russian Federation', paper presented at CREES, University of Birmingham, May 1998.

Lebed, A. (1995), *Za derzhavu obidno* (Moskva).

Levada, I. (1992), 'Social and Moral Aspects of the Crisis: their Sources and Consequences', in Ellman, M. and Kontorovich, V. (eds), *The Disintegration of the Soviet Economic System* (London and New York: Routledge) pp. 59–73.

Malle, S. (1996), 'Russian Entrepreneurship and Business in Transition: Towards the Re-Building of State Conglomerates', *Journal of International and Comparative Economics*, 20, pp. 37–64.

Mau, V. and Stupin, V. (1997), 'The Political Economy of Russian Regionalism', *Communist Economies and Economic Transformation*, 9:1, pp. 5–25.

Mikheyev, D. (1996), *Russia Transformed* (Indianapolis: Hudson Institute).

Morozova, T. (ed.) (1995), *Regionalnaja Ekonomika* (Moscow: Unity).

Moskovskie Novosti (Moscow, weekly).

O'Prey, K. (1995), *A Farewell to Arms?* (Washington, DC: The Brookings Institution Press).

OECD (1993), *FDI in Selected Central and Eastern European Countries and The New Independent States* (Paris: OECD).

Porter, M. (1985), *Competitive Advantage* (New York: Free Press).

Press Klub (Volgograd, irregular).

Radaev, V. (1994), 'Vneshneeconomicheskie motivy predprinimatelskij dejatelnosti', *Voprocy ekonomiky*, 7, pp. 63–87.

Radsinsky, E. (1997), *Stalin* (Moscow: Vagrius).

Rutland, P. (1996), 'Firms Trapped between the Past and the Future', *Transition*, 22 March, pp. 26–32.

Sakwa, R. (1996), *Russian Politics and Society* (London and New York: Routledge, 2nd edn).

Scase, R. (1997), 'The Role of Small Business in the Economic Transformation of Eastern Europe: Real but Relatively Unimportant?', *International Small Business Journal*, 16:1, pp. 13–22.

Sedov, K. K. (1996), 'Raspredelinie Nalogov Mezdu Zveniami Budzhetnoj Systemy', *Finansy*, no. 2, pp. 24–32.

Shulus, A. (1996), 'Subjekt malogo predprinimatelstva i sistema ego gosudarstvennoj podderzhki', *Rossijskij ekonomicheskij zhurnal*, 5–6, pp. 65–76.

Skidelsky, R. (1996), 'The State and Economy: Reflections on the Transition from Communism to Capitalism in Russia', in M. Mandelbaum (ed.), *Post-Communism: Four Perspectives* (New York: Council on Foreign Relations) pp. 77–101.

Skuratov, Y. (1998), 'La corruzione nella Russia di oggi e le vie per sconfiggerla', in *La criminalità transnazionale organizzata, Dal riciclaggio all'usura* (Turin: Società Editrice Internazionale) pp. 91–101.

Smith, H. (1990), *The New Russians* (New York: Random House).

Steinbeck, J. (1994[1949]), *A Russian Journal* (London: Minerva).

Suvorov, V. (1996), *Poslednia Respublika* (Moscow: TKO ACT).

Volgogradskaja Pravda (Volgograd, daily).

Volgogradskij Statisticheskij Sbornik (1997) (Volgograd).

Vorochalina, L. (1996), 'Finansovo-Kreditny mechnizm regulirovania malogo biznesa', *Voprosy ekonomiky*, 7, pp. 83–7.

Yergin, D. and Gustafson, T. (1993), *Russia 2010* (New York: Random House).

Index